Bible Sentences
FOR
Common Worship

SHARON SWAIN

First published in Great Britain in 1998
Society for Promoting Christian Knowledge
Holy Trinity Church
Marylebone Road
London NW1 4DU

British Cataloguing-in-Publication Data

A catalogue record for this book is available from the British Library

ISBN 0-281-05195-X

Typeset by Pioneer Associates, Perthshire
Printed in Malta by Interprint Ltd.

CONTENTS

CONTENTS

PREFACE

Bible Sentences for Common Worship offers all those who lead worship appropriate Bible sentences with which to open and close services which they conduct. The book allows the minister to choose sentences appropriate to the theme for the service, whether that is at some specific time in the Church's calendar, for example, Easter, or for something more general, say on the theme of Praise or Creation.

Throughout *Bible Sentences for Common Worship* the New Revised Standard Version (Anglicized Edition) is used, and sentences are taken from the Old and New Testament as well as from the Apocrypha. Sentences of the latter are often placed at the end of the Old Testament sections.

Bible Sentences for Common Worship is divided into three sections. Part One offers sentences for use throughout the Church's Year, from Advent to Pentecost and including Harvest. Part Two has sentences for use at occasional services, like Funerals, Weddings and Baptisms. Part Three is more generalized, with sentences offered to cover different themes: for example, Jesus, Praise, Unity etc.

The first person singular is rarely used in this book, instead the plural is preferred since the sentences are designed for use in public worship. Where possible the sentences are complete in themselves, but sometimes, rather than distort the text from the Bible, an indication of who is speaking is given in square brackets. For example:

[Jesus said] 'I am the Good Shepherd.' (John 10.14)

Occasionally, words or phrases that might not be helpful are indicated by the use of angled brackets. For example:

<Beloved,> let us love one another . . . (1 John 4.7)

Those leading worship can choose to include or to leave out these sections, as appropriate.

A carefully chosen Bible sentence to open or close an act of worship can weave the theme of the whole service together to form a harmonious pattern. *Bible Sentences for Common Worship* allows ministers flexibility and creativity in the conduct of worship, with sufficient material to offer extensive choice to last for a number of years.

PART ONE

The Church Year

ADVENT
to Christmas

Old Testament Prophecy: The Day of the Lord

Our God comes and does not keep silence, before him is a devouring fire, and a mighty tempest all around him. He calls to the heavens above and to the earth, that he may judge his people. (Psalm 50.3–4)

Rise up, O God, judge the earth; for all the nations belong to you! (Psalm 82.8)

Then shall all the trees of the forest sing for joy before the Lord; for he is coming, for he is coming to judge the earth. (Psalm 96.12b–13a)

Wail, for the day of the Lord is near; it will come like destruction from the Almighty! (Isaiah 13.6)

Alas for the day! For the day of the Lord is near, and as destruction from the Almighty it comes. (Joel 1.15)

The great day of the Lord is near, near and hastening fast; the sound of the day of the Lord is bitter. (Zephaniah 1.14)

Old Testament: God's Judgement Brings Salvation

He will judge the world with righteousness, and the peoples with his truth. (Psalm 96.13b)

Let the sea roar, and all that fills it; the world and those who live in it. Let the floods clap their hands; let the hills sing together for joy at the presence of the Lord, for he is coming to judge the earth. He will judge the world with righteousness, and the peoples with equity. (Psalm 98.7–9)

The people who walked in darkness have seen a great light; those who lived in a land of deep darkness – on them light has shined. (Isaiah 9.2)

A shoot shall come out from the stock of Jesse, and a branch shall grow out of his roots. The spirit of the Lord shall rest on him, the spirit of wisdom and understanding, the spirit of counsel and might, the spirit of knowledge and the fear of the Lord. (Isaiah 11.1–2)

'Every valley shall be lifted up, and every mountain and hill be made low; the uneven ground shall become level, and the rough places a plain. Then the glory of the Lord shall be revealed.' (Isaiah 40.4–5a)

A voice cries out: 'In the wilderness prepare the way of the Lord, make straight in the desert a highway for our God.' (Isaiah 40.3)

How beautiful upon the mountains are the feet of the messenger who announces peace, who brings good news, who announces salvation, who says to Zion, 'Your God reigns.' (Isaiah 52.7)

Thus says the Lord: Maintain justice, and do what is right, for soon my salvation will come, and my deliverance be revealed. (Isaiah 56.1)

Arise, shine; for your light has come, and the glory of the Lord has risen upon you. (Isaiah 60.1)

For darkness shall cover the earth, and thick darkness the peoples; but the Lord will arise upon you, and his glory will appear over you. (Isaiah 60.2)

The Lord has proclaimed to the end of the earth: Say to daughter Zion, 'See, your salvation comes.' (Isaiah 62.11)

Look! On the mountains the feet of one who brings good tidings, who proclaims peace! (Nahum 1.15a)

New Testament Prophecy: The Day of the Lord

'Even now the axe is lying at the root of the trees; every tree therefore that does not bear good fruit is cut down and thrown into the fire.' (Matthew 3.10)

'The time is fulfilled, and the kingdom of God has come near; repent and believe in the good news.' (Mark 1.15)

'Be alert at all times, praying that you may have the strength to escape all these things that will take place, and to stand before the Son of Man.' (Luke 21.36)

'Be on guard so that your hearts are not weighed down with dissipation and drunkenness and the worries of this life, and that day does not catch you unexpectedly, like a trap. For it will come upon all who live on the face of the whole earth.' (Luke 21.34–35)

It is now the moment for you to wake from sleep. For salvation is nearer to us now than when we became believers. (Romans 13.11)

The night is far gone, the day is near. Let us then lay aside the works of darkness and put on the armour of light. (Romans 13.12)

John the Baptist

In those days John the Baptist appeared in the wilderness of Judea, proclaiming, 'Repent, for the kingdom of heaven has come near.' (Matthew 3.1–2)

John the baptizer appeared in the wilderness, proclaiming a baptism of repentance for the forgiveness of sins. (Mark 1.4)

Now John was clothed with camel's hair, with a leather belt around his waist, and he ate locusts and wild honey. He proclaimed, 'The one who is more powerful than I is coming after me; I am not worthy to stoop down and untie the thong of his sandals. I have baptized you with water; but he will baptize you with the Holy Spirit.' (Mark 1.6–8)

CHRISTMAS
to Epiphany

Jesus: The Son of God

In the beginning was the Word, and the Word was with God, and the Word was God. He was in the beginning with God. (John 1.1–2)

The light shines in the darkness, and the darkness did not overcome it. (John 1.5)

And the Word became flesh and lived among us, and we have seen his glory, the glory as of a father's only son, full of grace and truth. (John 1.14)

'For God so loved the world that he gave his only Son, so that everyone who believes in him may not perish but may have eternal life.' (John 3.16)

'Indeed, God did not send the Son into the world to condemn the world, but in order that the world might be saved through him.' (John 3.17)

God's love was revealed among us in this way: God sent his only Son into the world so that we might live through him. (1 John 4.9)

We know that the Son of God has come and has given us understanding so that we may know him who is true; and we are in him who is true, in his Son Jesus Christ. He is the true God and eternal life. (1 John 5.20)

In this is love, not that we loved God but that he loved us and sent his Son to be the atoning sacrifice for our sins. (1 John 4.10)

Jesus: Birth

The Lord himself will give you a sign. Look, the young woman is with child and shall bear a son, and shall name him Immanuel. (Isaiah 7.14)

For a child has been born for us, a Son given to us; authority rests upon his shoulders; and he is named Wonderful Counsellor, Mighty God, Everlasting Father, Prince of Peace. (Isaiah 9.6)

But you, O Bethlehem of Ephrathah, who are one of the little clans of Judah, from you shall come forth for me one who is to rule in Israel, whose origin is from of old, from ancient days. (Micah 5.2)

'Look, the virgin shall conceive and bear a son, and they shall name him Emmanuel', which means, 'God is with us.' (Matthew 1.23)

'And you, Bethlehem, in the land of Judah, are by no means least among the rulers of Judah; for from you shall come a ruler who is to shepherd my people Israel.' (Matthew 2.6)

In the sixth month the angel Gabriel was sent by God to a town in Galilee called Nazareth, to a virgin engaged to a man whose name was Joseph, of the house of David. The virgin's name was Mary. (Luke 1.26–27)

And Mary said, 'My soul magnifies the Lord, and my spirit rejoices in God my Saviour, for he has looked with favour on the lowliness of his servant.' (Luke 1.46–48)

But the angel said to them, 'Do not be afraid; for see – I am bringing you good news of great joy for all the people: to you is born this day in the city of David a Saviour, who is the Messiah, the Lord.' (Luke 2.10–11)

And suddenly there was with the angel a multitude of the heavenly host, praising God and saying, 'Glory to God in the highest heaven, and on earth peace among those whom he favours!' (Luke 2.13–14)

When the angels had left them and gone into heaven, the shepherds said to one another, 'Let us go now to Bethlehem and see this thing that has taken place, which the Lord has made known to us.' (Luke 2.15)

They went with haste and found Mary and Joseph, and the child lying in the manger. (Luke 2.16)

Mary treasured all these words and pondered them in her heart. The shepherds returned, glorifying and praising God for all they had heard and seen, as it had been told them. (Luke 2.19–20)

EPIPHANY
to Ash Wednesday

Jesus: Good News to the Gentiles

From the rising of the sun to its setting my name is great among the nations, and in every place incense is offered to my name, and a pure offering, for my name is great among the nations, says the Lord of hosts. (Malachi 1.11)

Look towards the east, O Jerusalem, and see the joy that is coming to you from God. (Baruch 4.36)

Wise men from the East came to Jerusalem, asking, 'Where is the child who has been born king of the Jews? For we observed his star at its rising, and have come to pay him homage.' (Matthew 2.1b–2)

When they saw that the star had stopped, they were overwhelmed with joy. On entering the house, they saw the child with Mary his mother, and they knelt down and paid him homage. (Matthew 2.10–11a)

Jesus: Childhood

After eight days had passed, it was time to circumcise the child; and he was called Jesus, the name given by the angel before he was conceived in the womb. (Luke 2.21)

Guided by the Spirit, Simeon came into the temple; and when the parents brought in the child Jesus, to do for him what was customary under the law, Simeon took him in his arms and praised God, saying, 'Master, now you are dismissing your servant in peace, according to your word; for my eyes have seen your salvation.' (Luke 2.27–30)

The child grew and became strong, filled with wisdom; and the favour of God was upon him. (Luke 2.40)

And Jesus increased in wisdom and in years, and in divine and human favour. (Luke 2.52)

And the Word became flesh and lived among us, and we have seen his glory, the glory as of a father's only son, full of grace and truth. (John 1.14)

Jesus: Baptism

Jesus came from Galilee to John at the Jordan, to be baptized by him. (Matthew 3.13)

When Jesus had been baptized, just as he came up from the water, suddenly the heavens were opened to him and he saw the Spirit of God descending like a dove and alighting on him. (Matthew 3.16)

And a voice from heaven said, 'This is my Son, the Beloved, with whom I am well pleased.' (Matthew 3.17)

From the cloud came a voice that said, 'This is my Son, my Chosen; listen to him!' When the voice had spoken, Jesus was found alone. And they kept silent and in those days told no one any of the things they had seen. (Luke 9.35–36)

John testified to him and cried out, 'This was he of whom I said, "He who comes after me ranks ahead of me because he was before me." ' (John 1.15)

And John testified, 'I saw the Spirit descending from heaven like a dove, and it remained on him. I myself did not know him, but the one who sent me to baptize with water said to me, "He on whom you see the Spirit descend and remain is the one who baptizes with the Holy Spirit." And I myself have seen and have testified that this is the Son of God. ' (John 1.32–34)

Jesus: Ministry

Jesus went throughout Galilee, teaching in their synagogues and proclaiming the good news of the kingdom and curing every disease and every sickness among the people. (Matthew 4.23)

Now when Jesus had finished saying these things, the crowds were astounded at his teaching, for he taught them as one having authority, and not as their scribes. (Matthew 7.28–29)

When Jesus had come down from the mountain, great crowds followed him; and there was a leper who came to him and knelt before him, saying, 'Lord, if you choose, you can make me clean.' He stretched out his hand and touched him, saying, 'I do choose. Be made clean!' Immediately his leprosy was cleansed. (Matthew 8.1–3)

Jesus said to them, 'Follow me and I will make you fish for people.' And immediately they left their nets and followed him. (Mark 1.17)

Jesus went out again beside the lake; the whole crowd gathered around him, and he taught them. (Mark 2.13)

With many such parables he [Jesus] spoke the word to them, as they were able to hear it; he did not speak to them except in parables, but he explained everything in private to his disciples. (Mark 4.33–34)

They [the people] were astounded beyond measure, saying, 'He has done everything well; he even makes the deaf to hear and the mute to speak.' (Mark 7.37)

Jesus, full of the Holy Spirit, returned from the Jordan and was led by the Spirit in the wilderness, where for forty days he was tempted by the devil. (Luke 4.1–2a)

Then Jesus, filled with the power of the Spirit, returned to Galilee, and a report about him spread through all the surrounding country. He began to teach in their synagogues and was praised by everyone. (Luke 4.14–15)

Jesus and his disciples went into the Judean countryside, and he spent some time there with them and baptized. (John 3.22)

Then Jesus called the twelve together and gave them power and authority over all demons and to cure diseases, and he sent them out to proclaim the kingdom of God and to heal. (Luke 9.1–2)

Jesus said to them, 'Very truly, I tell you, I am the gate for the sheep.' (John 10.7)

Jesus: The Temptations

Then Jesus was led up by the Spirit into the wilderness to be tempted by the devil. (Matthew 4.1)

'Stay awake and pray that you may not come into the time of trial; the spirit indeed is willing, but the flesh is weak.' (Matthew 26.41)

He [Jesus] was in the wilderness for forty days, tempted by Satan; and he was with the wild beasts; and the angels waited on him. (Mark 1.13)

Jesus, full of the Holy Spirit, returned from the Jordan and was led by the Spirit in the wilderness, where for forty days he was tempted by the devil. (Luke 4.1–2a)

Christians Today: Waiting on God

The law of the Lord is perfect, reviving the soul; the decrees of the Lord are sure, making wise the simple. (Psalm 19.7)

The precepts of the Lord are right, rejoicing the heart; the commandment of the Lord is clear. (Psalm 19.8)

Hear my prayer, O Lord; let my cry come to you. Do not hide your face from me on the day of my distress. (Psalm 102.1–2a)

Seek the Lord and his strength; seek his presence continually. (Psalm 105.4)

The fear of the Lord is the beginning of wisdom; all those who practise it have a good understanding. (Psalm 111.10)

Happy are those who fear the Lord, who greatly delight in his commandments. (Psalm 112.1b)

Thus said the Lord God, the Holy One of Israel: in returning and rest you shall be saved; in quietness and in trust shall be your strength. (Isaiah 30.15)

Christians Today: Need for Self-examination

The sacrifice acceptable to God is a broken spirit; a broken and contrite heart, O God, you will not despise. (Psalm 51.17)

O Lord, you are our Father; we are the clay, and you are our potter; we are all the work of your hand. Do not be exceedingly angry, O Lord, and do not remember iniquity for ever. (Isaiah 64.8–9a)

Restore us to yourself, O Lord, that we may be restored; renew our days as of old. (Lamentations 5.21)

O Lord, look down from your holy dwelling, and consider us. Incline your ear, O Lord, and hear; open your eyes, O Lord, and see. (Baruch 2.16–17a)

The night is far gone, the day is near. Let us then lay aside the works of darkness and put on the armour of light. (Romans 13.12)

'Be alert at all times, praying that you may have the strength to escape all these things that will take place, and to stand before the Son of Man.' (Luke 21.36)

Christians Today: God's mercy

The Lord sits enthroned for ever, he has established his throne for judgement. He judges the world with righteousness; he judges the people with equity. (Psalm 9.7–8)

The Lord is merciful and gracious, slow to anger and abounding in steadfast love. (Psalm 103.8)

Great is your mercy, O Lord; give me life according to your justice. (Psalm 119.156)

The Lord is gracious and merciful, slow to anger and abounding in steadfast love. The Lord is good to all, and his compassion is over all that he has made. (Psalm 145.8–9)

The Lord waits to be gracious to you; therefore he will rise up to show mercy to you. For the Lord is a God of justice; blessed are all those who wait for him. (Isaiah 30.18)

To the Lord our God belong mercy and forgiveness, for we have rebelled against him, and have not obeyed the voice of the Lord our God by following his laws. (Daniel 9.9)

Jesus: The Welcome into Jerusalem

Rejoice greatly, O daughter Zion! Shout aloud, O daughter Jerusalem! Lo, your king comes to you; triumphant and victorious is he, humble and riding on a donkey, on a colt, the foal of a donkey. (Zechariah 9.9)

'Tell the daughter of Zion, Look, your king is coming to you, humble and mounted on a donkey, and on a colt, the foal of a donkey.' (Matthew 21.5)

'Hosanna to the Son of David! Blessed is the one who comes in the name of the Lord! Hosanna in the highest heaven!' (Matthew 21.9b)

The crowd that had come to the festival heard that Jesus was coming to Jerusalem. So they took branches of palm trees and went out to meet him, shouting, 'Hosanna! Blessed is the one who comes in the name of the Lord – the King of Israel!' (John 12.12–13)

Jesus found a young donkey and sat on it; as it is written: 'Do not be afraid, daughter of Zion. Look, your king is coming, sitting on a donkey's colt!' (John 12.14–15)

Jesus: The Last Supper

Jesus sent two disciples, saying to them, 'Go into the village ahead of you, and immediately you will find a donkey tied, and a colt with her; untie them and bring them to me. If anyone says anything to you, just say this, "The Lord needs them."' (Matthew 21.1b–3a)

Jesus sent Peter and John, saying, 'Go and prepare the Passover meal for us that we may eat it.' (Luke 22.8)

The Lord Jesus on the night when he was betrayed took a loaf of bread, and when he had given thanks, he broke it and said, 'This is my body that is for you. Do this in remembrance of me.' (1 Corinthians 11.23b–24)

In the same way he [Jesus] took the cup also, after supper, saying, 'This cup is the new covenant in my blood. Do this, as often as you drink it, in remembrance of me.' (1 Corinthians 11.25)

For as often as you eat this bread and drink the cup, you proclaim the Lord's death until he comes. (1 Corinthians 11.26)

'This is the bread that came down from heaven, not like that which your ancestors ate, and they died. But the one who eats this bread will live for ever.' (John 6.58)

[Jesus said] 'I give you a new commandment, that you love one another. Just as I have loved you, you also should love one another.' (John 13.34)

Jesus: In the Garden of Gethsemane

'Stay awake and pray that you may not come into the time of trial; the spirit indeed is willing, but the flesh is weak.' (Matthew 26.41)

Again he [Jesus] went away for the second time and prayed, 'My Father, if this cannot pass unless I drink it, your will be done.' (Matthew 26.42b)

'The hour is at hand, and the Son of Man is betrayed into the hands of sinners.' (Matthew 26.45b)

After Jesus had spoken these words, he looked up to heaven and said, 'Father, the hour has come; glorify your Son so that the Son may glorify you.' (John 17.1)

Jesus: Suffering and Death

Jesus answered, 'My kingdom is not from this world. If my kingdom were from this world, my followers would be fighting to keep me from being handed over to the Jews. But as it is, my kingdom is not from here.' (John 18.36)

Pilate asked him, 'So you are a king?' Jesus answered, 'You say that I am a king. For this I was born, and for this I came into the world, to testify to the truth. Everyone who belongs to the truth listens to my voice.' (John 18.37)

Pilate asked them, 'Shall I crucify your King?' The chief priests answered, 'We have no king but the emperor.' Then he handed him over to them to be crucified. (John 19.15b–16)

Jesus said, 'Father, forgive them; for they do not know what they are doing.' (Luke 23.34)

He [the criminal] said, 'Jesus, remember me when you come into your kingdom.' He replied, 'Truly I tell you, today you will be with me in Paradise.' (Luke 23.42–43)

Then Jesus, crying with a loud voice, said, 'Father, into your hands I commend my spirit.' Having said this, he breathed his last. (Luke 23.46)

It was now about noon, and darkness came over the whole land until three in the afternoon, while the sun's light failed; and the curtain of the temple was torn in two. (Luke 23.44–45)

Now when the centurion and those with him, who were keeping watch over Jesus, saw the earthquake and what took place, they were terrified and said, 'Truly this man was God's Son!' (Matthew 27.54)

Jesus: The Meaning of His death

He was despised and rejected by others; a man of suffering and acquainted with infirmity; and as one from whom others hide their faces he was despised, and we held him of no account. (Isaiah 53.3)

Surely he has borne our infirmities and carried our diseases; yet we accounted him stricken, struck down by God, and afflicted. But he was wounded for our transgressions, crushed for our iniquities. (Isaiah 53.4–5a)

He was oppressed, and he was afflicted, yet he did not open his mouth; like a lamb that is led to the slaughter, and like a sheep that before its shearers is silent, so he did not open his mouth. (Isaiah 53.7)

He poured out himself to death, and was numbered with the transgressors; yet he bore the sin of many, and made intercession for the transgressors. (Isaiah 53.12b)

The Son of Man came not to be served but to serve, and to give his life a ransom for many.' (Matthew 20.28)

'Unless a grain of wheat falls into the earth and dies, it remains just a single grain; but if it dies, it bears much fruit.' (John 12.24)

God proves his love for us in that while we still were sinners Christ died for us. (Romans 5.8)

For just as by the one man's disobedience the many were made sinners, so by the one man's obedience the many will be made righteous. (Romans 5.19)

Do you not know that all of us who have been baptized into Christ Jesus were baptized into his death? Therefore we have been buried with him by baptism into death. (Romans 6.3)

He who did not withhold his own Son, but gave him up for all of us, will he not with him also give us everything else? (Romans 8.32)

. . . Christ Jesus, who, though he was in the form of God, did not regard equality with God as something to be exploited, but emptied himself, taking the form of a slave, being born in human likeness. And being found in human form, he humbled himself and became obedient to the point of death – even death on a cross. (Philippians 2.5b–8)

EASTER
to Ascension

Prophecy

Sing for joy, O heavens, and exult, O earth; break forth, O mountains, into singing! For the Lord has comforted his people, and will have compassion on his suffering ones. (Isaiah 49.13)

'The Son of Man is to be betrayed into human hands, and they will kill him, and three days after being killed, he will rise again.' (Mark 9.31)

'Thus it is written, that the Messiah is to suffer and to rise from the dead on the third day.' (Luke 24.46)

Jesus answered them, 'Destroy this temple, and in three days I will raise it up.' (John 2.19)

Jesus: Resurrection Appearances

After the sabbath, as the first day of the week was dawning, Mary Magdalene and the other Mary went to see the tomb. (Matthew 28.1)

And very early on the first day of the week, when the sun had risen, they [the women] went to the tomb.

They had been saying to one another, 'Who will roll away the stone for us from the entrance to the tomb?' When they looked up, they saw that the stone, which was very large, had already been rolled back. (Mark 16.2–4)

On the first day of the week, at early dawn, they [the women] came to the tomb, taking the spices that they had prepared. They found the stone rolled away from the tomb, but when they went in, they did not find the body. (Luke 24.1–2)

So he [Jesus] went in to stay with them. When he was at table with them, he took bread, blessed and broke it, and gave it to them. Then their eyes were opened, and they recognized him. (Luke 24.29b–3la)

Then they [the two men] told what had happened on the road, and how he [Jesus] had been made known to them in the breaking of the bread. (Luke 24.35)

Mary Magdalene went and announced to the disciples, 'I have seen the Lord.' (John 20.18a)

When it was evening on that day, the first day of the week, and the doors of the house where the disciples had met were locked for fear of the Jews, Jesus came and stood among them and said, 'Peace be with you.' (John 20.19)

Then the disciples rejoiced when they saw the Lord. Jesus said to them again, 'Peace be with you.' (John 20.20b–21b)

After these things Jesus showed himself again to the disciples by the Sea of Tiberias. (John 21.1)

Just after daybreak, Jesus stood on the beach; but the disciples did not know that it was Jesus. (John 21.4)

Jesus said to them, 'Come and have breakfast.' Now none of the disciples dared to ask him, 'Who are you?' because they knew it was the Lord. Jesus came and took the bread and gave it to them, and did the same with the fish. (John 21.12–13)

After his suffering he presented himself alive to them by many convincing proofs, appearing to them over the course of forty days and speaking about the kingdom of God. (Acts 1.3)

The Meaning of the Resurrection

'Was it not necessary that the Messiah should suffer these things and then enter into his glory?' (Luke 24.26)

Jesus said to them, 'I am the bread of life. Whoever comes to me will never be hungry, and whoever believes in me will never be thirsty.' (John 6.35)

'This is indeed the will of my Father, that all who see the Son and believe in him may have eternal life; and I will raise them up on the last day.' (John 6.40)

[Jesus said] 'l am the good shepherd. I know my own and my own know me, just as the Father knows me and I know the Father. And I lay down my life for the sheep.' (John 10.14–15)

Jesus said to him, 'I am the way, and the truth, and the life. No one comes to the Father except through me.' (John 14.6)

Christ has been raised from the dead, the first fruits of those who have died. For since death came through a human being, the resurrection of the dead has also come through a human being. (1 Corinthians 15.20–21)

For as all die in Adam, so all will be made alive in Christ. (1 Corinthians 15.22)

The saying is sure and worthy of full acceptance, that Christ Jesus came into the world to save sinners. (1 Timothy 1.15)

For there is one God; there is also one mediator between God and humankind, Christ Jesus, himself human, who gave himself a ransom for all. (1 Timothy 2.5–6a)

We have an advocate with the Father, Jesus Christ the righteous; and he is the atoning sacrifice for our sins, and not for ours only but also for the sins of the whole world. (1 John 2.1b–2)

In this is love, not that we loved God but that he loved us and sent his Son to be the atoning sacrifice for our sins. (1 John 4.10)

ASCENSION
to Pentecost

[Jesus said] 'And remember, I am with you always, to the end of the age.' (Matthew 28.20b)

Then he led them out as far as Bethany, and, lifting up his hands, he blessed them. While he was blessing them, he withdrew from them and was carried up into heaven. And they worshipped him, and returned to Jerusalem with great joy; and they were continually in the temple blessing God. (Luke 24.50–52)

[Jesus said] 'I came from the Father and have come into the world; again, I am leaving the world and am going to the Father.' (John 16.28)

While he was going and they were gazing up towards heaven, suddenly two men in white robes stood by them. 'Men of Galilee, why do you stand looking up towards heaven? This Jesus, who has been taken up from you into heaven, will come in the same way as you saw him go into heaven.' (Acts 1.10–11)

We know that Christ, being raised from the dead, will never die again; death no longer has dominion over him. (Romans 6.9)

It is Christ Jesus, who died, yes, who was raised, who is at the right hand of God, who indeed intercedes for us. (Romans 8.34b)

The Disciples: Receiving the Holy Spirit

[Jesus said] 'You will receive power when the Holy Spirit has come upon you; and you will be my witnesses in Jerusalem, in all Judea and Samaria, and to the ends of the earth.' (Acts 1.8)

When the day of Pentecost had come, they were all together in one place. And suddenly from heaven there came a sound like the rush of a violent wind, and it filled the entire house where they were sitting. (Acts 2.1–2)

Divided tongues, as of fire, appeared among them, and a tongue rested on each of them. All of them were filled with the Holy Spirit and began to speak in other languages, as the Spirit gave them ability. (Acts 2.3–4)

The Disciples: Signs and Wonders

Peter said to them, 'Repent, and be baptized every one of you in the name of Jesus Christ so that your sins may be forgiven; and you will receive the gift of the Holy Spirit. For the promise is for you, for your children, and for all who are far away, everyone whom the Lord our God calls to him.' (Acts 2.38)

Awe came upon everyone, because many wonders and signs were being done by the apostles. (Acts 2.43)

All who believed were together and had all things in common; they would sell their possessions and goods and distribute the proceeds to all, as any had need. (Acts 2.44–45)

Day by day, as they spent much time together in the temple, they broke bread at home and ate their food with glad and generous hearts, praising God and having the goodwill of the people. And day by day the Lord added to their number those who were being saved. (Acts 2.46–47)

Now the whole group of those who believed were of one heart and soul, and no one claimed private ownership of any possessions, but everything they owned was held in common. (Acts 4.32)

With great power the apostles gave their testimony to the resurrection of the Lord Jesus, and great grace was upon them all. (Acts 4.33)

Old Testament

As long as the earth endures, seedtime and harvest, cold and heat, summer and winter, day and night, shall not cease. (Genesis 8.22)

You shall observe the festival of harvest, of the first fruits of your labour, of what you sow in the field. You shall observe the festival of ingathering at the end of the year, when you gather in from the field the fruit of your labour. (Exodus 23.16)

The choicest of the first fruits of your ground you shall bring into the house of the Lord your God. (Exodus 23.19)

The best of the first fruits of your ground you shall bring to the house of the Lord your God. (Exodus 34.26a)

For six days you shall work, but on the seventh day you shall rest; even in ploughing time and in harvest you shall rest. (Exodus 34.21)

You shall eat your fill and bless the Lord your God for the good land that he has given you. (Deuteronomy 8.10)

The river of God is full of water; you provide the people with grain, for so you have prepared it. You water its furrows abundantly, settling its ridges, softening it with showers, and blessing its growth. (Psalm 65.9b–10)

The earth has yielded its increase; God, our God, has blessed us. May God continue to bless us; let all the ends of the earth revere him. (Psalm 67.6–7)

The Lord will give what is good, and our land will yield its increase. (Psalm 85.12)

From your lofty abode you water the mountains; the earth is satisfied with the fruit of your work. (Psalm 104.13)

You cause the grass to grow for the cattle, and plants for people to use, to bring forth food from the earth. (Psalm 104.14)

The trees of the field shall yield their fruit, and the earth shall yield its increase. (Ezekiel 34.27a)

New Testament

'Do not work for the food that perishes, but for the food that endures for eternal life, which the Son of Man will give you.' (John 6.27a)

Then Jesus said to them, 'Very truly, I tell you, it was not Moses who gave you the bread from heaven, but it is my Father who gives you the true bread from heaven.' (John 6.32)

God is able to provide you with every blessing in abundance, so that by always having enough of everything, you may share abundantly in every good work. (2 Corinthians 9.8)

PART TWO

Occasional Services

BAPTISM AND CONFIRMATION

Old Testament: God's People

The Lord is our God, the Lord alone. You shall love the Lord your God with all your heart, and with all your soul, and with all your might. Keep these words that I am commanding you today in your heart. Recite them to your children and talk about them when you are at home and when you are away, when you lie down and when you rise. (Deuteronomy 6.4–7)

Commit your way to the Lord; trust in him, and he will act. (Psalm 37.5)

New Testament: Being Baptized into Christ

'For God so loved the world that he gave his only Son, so that everyone who believes in him may not perish but may have eternal life.' (John 3.16)

All of us who have been baptized into Christ Jesus were baptized into his death. Therefore we have been buried with him by baptism into death, so that, just as Christ was raised from the dead by the glory of the Father, so we too might walk in newness of life. (Romans 6.3–4)

If we have died with Christ, we believe that we will also live with him. (Romans 6.8)

So if anyone is in Christ, there is a new creation: everything old has passed away; see, everything has become new! (2 Corinthians 5.17)

As you therefore have received Christ Jesus the Lord, continue to live your lives in him, rooted and built up in him and established in the faith, just as you were taught, abounding in thanksgiving. (Colossians 2.6–7)

Set your minds on things that are above, not on things that are on earth, for you have died, and your life is hidden with Christ in God. (Colossians 3.2–3)

Clothe yourselves with love, which binds everything together in perfect harmony. And let the peace of Christ rule in your hearts, to which indeed you were called in the one body. (Colossians 3.14–15)

If we have died with him, we will also live with him; if we endure, we will also reign with him; if we deny him, he will also deny us; if we are faithless, he remains faithful. (2 Timothy 2.11b–13a)

God abides in those who confess that Jesus is the Son of God, and they abide in God. So we have known and believe the love that God has for us. (1 John 4.15–16)

Everyone who believes that Jesus is the Christ has been born of God. (1 John 5.1a)

Instructions for New Christians

'Do not work for the food that perishes, but for the food that endures for eternal life, which the Son of Man will give you. For it is on him that God the Father has set his seal.' (John 6.27)

Jesus said to them, 'I am the bread of life. Whoever comes to me will never be hungry, and whoever believes in me will never be thirsty.' (John 6.35)

Jesus said to them, 'Very truly, I tell you, unless you eat the flesh of the Son of Man and drink his blood, you have no life in you. Those who eat my flesh and drink my blood have eternal life, and I will raise them up on the last day; for my flesh is true food and my blood is true drink. Those who eat my flesh and drink my blood abide in me, and I in them.' (John 6.53–56)

Jesus spoke to them, saying, 'I am the light of the world. Whoever follows me will never walk in darkness but will have the light of life.' (John 8.12)

The Lord Jesus on the night when he was betrayed took a loaf of bread, and when he had given thanks, he broke it and said, 'This is my body that is for you. Do this in remembrance of me.' In the same way he took the cup also, after supper, saying, 'This cup is the new covenant in my blood. Do this, as often as you drink it, in remembrance of me.' (1 Corinthians 11.23b–25)

For as often as you eat this bread and drink the cup, you proclaim the Lord's death until he comes. (1 Corinthians 11.26)

Old Testament

Your steadfast love, O Lord, extends to the heavens, your faithfulness to the clouds. Your righteousness is like the mighty mountains, your judgements are like the great deep. (Psalm 36.5–6a)

The Lord upholds all who are falling, and raises up all who are bowed down. The eyes of all look to you. (Psalm 145.14–15a)

Then the Lord God will wipe away the tears from all faces, and the disgrace of his people he will take away from all the earth, for the Lord has spoken. (Isaiah 25.8b)

The grass withers, the flower fades; but the word of our God will stand for ever. (Isaiah 40.8)

The steadfast love of the Lord never ceases, his mercies never come to an end; they are new every morning; great is your faithfulness. (Lamentations 3.22–23)

The Lord is good to those who wait for him, to the soul that seeks him. It is good that one should wait quietly for the salvation of the Lord. (Lamentations 3.25–26)

I myself will be the shepherd of my sheep, and I will make them lie down, says the Lord God. I will seek the lost, and I will bring back the strayed, and I will bind up the injured, and I will strengthen the weak. (Ezekiel 34.15–16a)

You are my sheep, the sheep of my pasture, and I am your God, says the Lord God. (Ezekiel 34.31)

The souls of the righteous are in the hand of God, and no torment will ever touch them. (Wisdom of Solomon 3.1)

New Testament

People were bringing little children to him in order that he might touch them; and the disciples spoke sternly to them. But when Jesus saw this, he was indignant and said to them, "Let the little children come to me; do not stop them; for it is to such as these that the kingdom of God belongs."' (Mark 10.13–14)

'Very truly, I tell you, anyone who hears my word and believes him who sent me has eternal life, and does not come under judgement, but has passed from death to life.' (John 5.24)

Jesus said to them, 'I am the bread of life. Whoever comes to me will never be hungry, and whoever believes in me will never be thirsty.' (John 6.35)

'Those who eat my flesh and drink my blood have eternal life, and I will raise them up on the last day; for my flesh is true food and my blood is true drink. Those who eat my flesh and drink my blood abide in me, and I in them.' (John 6.54–56)

Jesus said <to her>, 'I am the resurrection and the life. Those who believe in me, even though they die, will live, and everyone who lives and believes in me will never die.' (John 11.25–26)

'Do not let your hearts be troubled. Believe in God, believe also in me. In my Father's house there are many dwelling-places. If it were not so, would I have told you that I go to prepare a place for you? And if I go and prepare a place for you, I will come again and will take you to myself, so that where I am, there you may be also.' (John 14.1–3)

We know that Christ, being raised from the dead, will never die again; death no longer has dominion over him. The death he died, he died to sin, once for all; but the life he lives, he lives to God. So you also must consider yourselves dead to sin and alive to God in Christ Jesus. (Romans 6.9–11)

Who will separate us from the love of Christ? Will hardship, or distress, or persecution, or famine, or nakedness, or peril, or sword? (Romans 8.35)

Neither death, nor life, nor angels, nor rulers, nor things present, nor things to come, nor powers, nor height, nor depth, nor anything else in all creation, will be able to separate us from the love of God in Christ Jesus our Lord. (Romans 8.38–39)

Christ has been raised from the dead, the first fruits of those who have died. For since death came through a human being, the resurrection of the dead has also come through a human being; for as all die in Adam, so all will be made alive in Christ. (1 Corinthians 15.20–22)

The sting of death is sin, and the power of sin is the law. But thanks be to God who gives us the victory through our Lord Jesus Christ. (1 Corinthians 15.56–57)

But we have this treasure in clay jars, so that it may be made clear that this extraordinary power belongs to God and does not come from us. We are afflicted in every way, but not crushed; perplexed, but not driven to despair; persecuted, but not forsaken; struck down, but not destroyed; always carrying in the body the death of Jesus, so that the life of Jesus may also be made visible in our bodies. (2 Corinthians 4.7–10)

[Jesus said] 'My grace is sufficient for you, for power is made perfect in weakness.' (2 Corinthians 12.9a)

Therefore I am content with weaknesses, insults, hardships, persecutions, and calamities for the sake of Christ; for whenever I am weak, then I am strong. (2 Corinthians 12.10)

[St Paul says] I pray that, according to the riches of his glory, he may grant that you may be strengthened in your inner being with power through his Spirit, and that Christ may dwell in your hearts through faith, as you are being rooted and grounded in love. (Ephesians 3.16–17)

[St Paul says] I pray that you may have the power to comprehend, with all the saints, what is the breadth and length and height and depth, and to know the love of Christ that surpasses knowledge, so that you may be filled with all the fullness of God. (Ephesians 3.18–19)

We believe that Jesus died and rose again, even so, through Jesus, God will bring with him those who have died. (1 Thessalonians 4.14)

Blessed be the God and Father of our Lord Jesus Christ! By his great mercy he has given us a new birth into a living hope through the resurrection of Jesus Christ from the dead, and into an inheritance that is imperishable, undefiled, and unfading, kept in heaven for you. (1 Peter 1.3–5)

God is love, and those who abide in love abide in God, and God abides in them. (1 John 4.16b)

They will hunger no more, and thirst no more; the sun will not strike them, nor any scorching heat; for the Lamb at the centre of the throne will be their shepherd, and he will guide them to springs of the water of life, and God will wipe away every tear from their eyes. (Revelation 7.16–17)

HOLY COMMUNION

The Lord's Supper

While they were eating, Jesus took a loaf of bread, and after blessing it he broke it, gave it to the disciples, and said, 'Take, eat; this is my body.' Then he took a cup, and after giving thanks he gave it to them, saying, 'Drink from it, all of you; for this is my blood of the covenant, which is poured out for many for the forgiveness of sins.' (Matthew 26.26–28)

Then he took a cup, and after giving thanks he said, 'Take this and divide it among yourselves; for I tell you that from now on I will not drink of the fruit of the vine until the kingdom of God comes.' Then he took a loaf of bread, and when he had given thanks, he broke it and gave it to them, saying, 'This is my body, which is given for you. Do this in remembrance of me.' (Luke 22.17–19)

And he did the same with the cup after supper, saying, 'This cup that is poured out for you is the new covenant in my blood.' (Luke 22.20)

The Lord Jesus on the night when he was betrayed took a loaf of bread, and when he had given thanks, he broke it and said, 'This is my body that is for you. Do this in remembrance of me.' In the same way he took the cup also, after supper, saying, 'This cup is the new covenant in my blood. Do this, as often as you drink it, in remembrance of me.' (1 Corinthians 11.23b–25)

For as often as you eat this bread and drink the cup, you proclaim the Lord's death until he comes. (1 Corinthians 11.26)

Whoever, therefore, eats the bread or drinks the cup of the Lord in an unworthy manner will be answerable for the body and blood of the Lord. Examine yourselves, and only then eat of the bread and drink of the cup. For all who eat and drink without discerning the body, eat and drink judgement against themselves. (1 Corinthians 11.27–29)

So he [Jesus] went in to stay with them [the two men]. When he was at table with them, he took bread, blessed and broke it, and gave it to them. Then their eyes were opened, and they recognized him. (Luke 24.29b–31a)

Then they told what had happened on the road, and how he had been made known to them in the breaking of the bread. (Luke 24.35)

Jesus: The Living Bread

Jesus said to them, 'I am the bread of life. Whoever comes to me will never be hungry, and whoever believes in me will never be thirsty.' (John 6.35)

'I am the bread of life. Your ancestors ate the manna in the wilderness, and they died. This is the bread that comes from heaven, so that one may eat of it and not die.' (John 6.48–50)

'I am the living bread that came down from heaven. Whoever eats of this bread will live for ever; and the bread that I will give for the life of the world is my flesh.' (John 6.51)

Jesus said to them, 'Very truly, I tell you, unless you eat the flesh of the Son of Man and drink his blood, you have no life in you. Those who eat my flesh and drink my blood have eternal life, and I will raise them up on the last day; for my flesh is true food and my blood is true drink. Those who eat my flesh and drink my blood abide in me, and I in them.' (John 6.53–56)

'This is the bread that came down from heaven, not like that which your ancestors ate, and they died. But the one who eats this bread will live for ever.' (John 6.58)

The cup of blessing that we bless, is it not a sharing in the blood of Christ? The bread that we break, is it not a sharing in the body of Christ? Because there is one bread, we who are many are one body, for we all partake of the one bread. (1 Corinthians 10.16–17)

MARRIAGE

'From the beginning of creation, "God made them male and female." "For this reason a man shall leave his father and mother and be joined to his wife, and the two shall become one flesh." So they are no longer two, but one flesh. Therefore what God has joined together, let no one separate.' (Mark 10.6–9)

[Jesus said] 'As the Father has loved me, so I have loved you; abide in my love. If you keep my commandments, you will abide in my love, just as I have kept my Father's commandments and abide in his love.' (John 15.9–10)

Love is patient; love is kind; love is not envious or boastful or arrogant or rude. It does not insist on its own way; it is not irritable or resentful; it does not rejoice in wrongdoing, but rejoices in the truth. It bears all things, believes all things, hopes all things, endures all things. (1 Corinthians 13.4–7)

Love never ends. But as for prophecies, they will come to an end; as for tongues, they will cease; as for knowledge, it will come to an end. (1 Corinthians 13.8)

Let love be genuine; hate what is evil, hold fast to what is good; love one another with mutual affection; outdo one another in showing honour. (Romans 12.9–10)

48

Therefore be imitators of God, <as beloved children,> and live in love, as Christ loved us and gave himself up for us, a fragrant offering and sacrifice to God. (Ephesians 5.1–2)

Live as children of light – for the fruit of the light is found in all that is good and right and true. (Ephesians 5.8b–9)

Be careful then how you live, not as unwise people but as wise, making the most of the time. (Ephesians 5.15–16a)

Be subject to one another out of reverence for Christ. (Ephesians 5.21)

Be strong in the Lord and in the strength of his power. Put on the whole armour of God, so that you may be able to stand against the wiles of the devil. (Ephesians 6.10–11)

As God's chosen ones, holy and beloved, clothe yourselves with compassion, kindness, humility, meekness, and patience. (Colossians 3.12)

<Beloved,> let us love one another, because love is from God; everyone who loves is born of God and knows God. (1 John 4.7)

<Beloved,> since God loved us so much, we also ought to love one another. No one has ever seen God; if we love one another, God lives in us, and his love is perfected in us. (1 John 4.11–12)

God abides in those who confess that Jesus is the Son of God, and they abide in God. So we have known and believe the love that God has for us. (1 John 4.15–16a)

God is love, and those who abide in love abide in God, and God abides in them. (1 John 4.16b)

PART THREE

Themes

BELIEF

Old Testament

The Lord is your keeper; the Lord is your shade at your right hand. The sun shall not strike you by day, nor the moon by night. The Lord will keep you from all evil; he will keep your life. (Psalm 121.5–7)

God is our refuge and strength, a very present help in trouble. (Psalm 46.1)

The Lord your God you shall fear; him you shall serve, and by his name alone you shall swear. (Deuteronomy 6.13)

You are great, O Lord God; for there is no one like you, and there is no God besides you, according to all that we have heard. (2 Samuel 7.22)

New Testament

'For everyone who asks receives, and everyone who searches finds, and for everyone who knocks, the door will be opened.' (Matthew 7.8)

peace with God through our Lord Jesus Christ, through whom we have obtained access to this
which we stand; and we boast in our hope of sharing the glory of God. (Romans 5.1–2)

God's love has been poured into our hearts through the Holy Spirit that has been given to us. (Romans 5.5b)

For whoever has died is freed from sin. But if we have died with Christ, we believe that we will also live with him. (Romans 6.7–8)

The wages of sin is death, but the free gift of God is eternal life in Christ Jesus our Lord. (Romans 6.23)

Neither death, nor life, nor angels, nor rulers, nor things present, nor things to come, nor powers, nor height, nor depth, nor anything else in all creation, will be able to separate us from the love of God in Christ Jesus our Lord. (Romans 8.38–39)

Just as we have borne the image of the man of dust, we will also bear the image of the man of heaven. (1 Corinthians 15.49)

God abides in those who confess that Jesus is the Son of God, and they abide in God. So we have known and believe the love that God has for us. (1 John 4.15–16)

Everyone who believes that Jesus is the Christ has been born of God. (1 John 5.1a)

God's love was revealed among us in this way: God sent his only Son into the world so that we might live through him. (1 John 4.9)

'For God so loved the world that he gave his only Son, so that everyone who believes in him may not perish but may have eternal life.' (John 3.16)

'Indeed, God did not send the Son into the world to condemn the world, but in order that the world might be saved through him.' (John 3.17)

So those who welcomed his [Peter's] message were baptized, and that day about three thousand persons were added. They devoted themselves to the apostles' teaching and fellowship, to the breaking of bread and the prayers. (Acts 2.41–42)

Awe came upon everyone, because many wonders and signs were being done by the apostles. All who believed were together and had all things in common; they would sell their possessions and goods and distribute the proceeds to all, as any had need. (Acts 2.43–45)

Day by day, as they spent much time together in the temple, they broke bread at home and ate their food with glad and generous hearts, praising God and having the goodwill of all the people. And day by day the Lord added to their number those who were being saved. (Acts 2.46–47)

When they had prayed, the place in which they were gathered together was shaken; and they were all filled with the Holy Spirit and spoke the word of God with boldness. (Acts 4.31)

Now the whole group of those who believed were of one heart and soul, and no one claimed private ownership of any possessions, but everything they owned was held in common. (Acts 4.32)

With great power the apostles gave their testimony to the resurrection of the Lord Jesus, and great grace was upon them all. There was not a needy person among them, for as many as owned lands or houses sold them and brought the proceeds of what was sold. They laid it at the apostles' feet, and it was distributed to each as any had need. (Acts 4.33–35)

Every day in the temple and at home they did not cease to teach and proclaim Jesus as the Messiah. (Acts 5.42)

When they believed Philip, who was proclaiming the good news about the kingdom of God and the name of Jesus Christ, they were baptized, both men and women. (Acts 8.12)

Now you are the body of Christ and individually members of it. (1 Corinthians 12.27)

Indeed, the body does not consist of one member but of many. (1 Corinthians 12.14)

If one member suffers, all suffer together with it; if one member is honoured, all rejoice together with it. (1 Corinthians 12.26)

God has appointed in the church first apostles, second prophets, third teachers; then deeds of power, then gifts of healing, forms of assistance, forms of leadership, various kinds of tongues. (1 Corinthians 12.28)

CREATION

Old Testament

In the beginning when God created the heavens and the earth, the earth was a formless void and darkness covered the face of the deep, while a wind from God swept over the face of the waters. (Genesis 1.1–2)

God made the wild animals of the earth of every kind, and the cattle of every kind, and everything that creeps upon the ground of every kind. And God saw that it was good. (Genesis 1.25)

So God created humankind in his image, in the image of God he created them; male and female he created them. (Genesis 1.27)

God saw everything that he had made, and indeed, it was very good. (Genesis 1.31)

Thus the heavens and the earth were finished, and all their multitude. And on the seventh day God finished the work that he had done, and he rested on the seventh day from all the work that he had done. (Genesis 2.1–2)

God blessed the seventh day and hallowed it, because on it God rested from all the work that he had done in creation. (Genesis 2.3)

The Lord God formed man from the dust of the ground, and breathed into his nostrils the breath of life; and the man became a living being. And the Lord God planted a garden in Eden, in the east; and there he put the man whom he had formed. (Genesis 2.7–8)

The Lord God formed every animal of the field and every bird of the air, and brought them to the man to see what he would call them; and whatever the man called each living creature, that was its name. (Genesis 2.19)

'You are the Lord, you alone; you have made heaven, the heaven of heavens, with all their host, the earth and all that is on it, the seas and all that is in them. To all of them you give life, and the host of heaven worships you.' (Nehemiah 9.6)

Surely God is great, and we do not know him; the number of his years is unsearchable. For he draws up the drops of water; he distils his mist in rain, which the skies pour down and drop upon mortals abundantly. (Job 36.26–28)

God thunders wondrously with his voice; he does great things that we cannot comprehend. For to the snow he says, 'Fall on the earth'; and the shower of rain, his heavy shower of rain, serves as a sign on everyone's hand, so that all whom he has made may know it. (Job 37.5–7)

By the breath of God ice is given, and the broad waters are frozen fast. He loads the thick cloud with moisture; the clouds scatter his lightning. They turn round and round by his guidance, to accomplish all that he commands them on the face of the habitable world. (Job 37.10–12)

The heavens are telling the glory of God; and the firmament proclaims his handiwork. (Psalm 19.1)

The earth is the Lord's and all that is in it, the world, and those who live in it. (Psalm 24.1)

By the word of the Lord the heavens were made, and all their host by the breath of his mouth. (Psalm 33.6)

The Lord is king, he is robed in majesty; the Lord is robed, he is girded with strength. He has established the world; it shall never be moved. (Psalm 93.1)

Whatever the Lord pleases he does, in heaven and on earth, in the seas and all deeps. He it is who makes the clouds rise at the end of the earth; he makes lightnings for the rain and brings out the wind from the storehouses. (Psalm 135.6–7)

Praise him, you highest heavens, and you waters above the heavens! Let them praise the name of the Lord, for he commanded and they were created. (Psalm 148.4–5)

DISCIPLESHIP

Old Testament

But know that the Lord has set apart the faithful for himself. (Psalm 4.3a)

The Lord redeems the life of his servants; none of those who take refuge in him will be condemned. (Psalm 34.22)

The Lord loves justice; he will not forsake his faithful ones. (Psalm 37.28)

Trust in the Lord for ever, for in the Lord God you have an everlasting rock. (Isaiah 26.4)

Seek the Lord your God, and you will find him if you search after him with all your heart and soul. (Deuteronomy 4.29)

A highway shall be there, and it shall be called the Holy Way; the unclean shall not travel on it, but it shall be for God's people; no traveller, not even fools, shall go astray. (Isaiah 35.8)

Those who wait for the Lord shall renew their strength, they shall mount up with wings like eagles, they shall run and not be weary, they shall walk and not faint. (Isaiah 40.31)

The Lord takes pleasure in those who fear him, in those who hope in his steadfast love. (Psalm 147.11)

You are a people holy to the Lord your God; the Lord your God has chosen you out of all the peoples on earth to be his people, his treasured possession. (Deuteronomy 7.6)

You shall fear the Lord your God; him alone you shall worship; to him you shall hold fast, and by his name you shall swear. He is your praise; he is your God, who has done for you these great and awesome things that your own eyes have seen. (Deuteronomy 10.20–21)

The fear of the Lord is the beginning of wisdom, and the knowledge of the Holy One is insight. (Proverbs 9.10)

The Lord is far from the wicked, but he hears the prayer of the righteous. (Proverbs 15.29)

The name of the Lord is a strong tower; the righteous run into it and are safe. (Proverbs 18.10)

Every word of God proves true; he is a shield to those who take refuge in him. (Proverbs 30.5)

New Testament: Citizens of the Kingdom

'You are those who have stood by me in my trials; and I confer on you, just as my Father has conferred on me, a kingdom, so that you may eat and drink at my table in my kingdom.' (Luke 22.28–30a)

You are no longer strangers and aliens, but you are citizens with the saints and also members of the household of God, built upon the foundation of the apostles and prophets, with Christ Jesus himself as the cornerstone. (Ephesians 2.19–20)

Once you were darkness, but now in the Lord you are light. Live as children of light – for the fruit of the light is found in all that is good and right and true. (Ephesians 5.8–9)

'Whoever serves me must follow me, and where I am, there will my servant be also. Whoever serves me, the Father will honour.' (John 12.26)

If we say that we have fellowship with him while we are walking in darkness, we lie and do not do what is true; but if we walk in the light as he himself is in the light, we have fellowship with one another, and the blood of Jesus his Son cleanses us from all sin. (1 John 1.6–7)

As servants of God, live as free people, yet do not use your freedom as a pretext for evil. (1 Peter 2.16)

Beloved, we are God's children now; what we will be has not yet been revealed. What we do know is this: when he is revealed, we will be like him, for we will see him as he is. (1 John 3.2)

Everyone who believes that Jesus is the Christ has been born of God. (1 John 5.1a)

Citizens of the Kingdom: Dead to Sin

If we say that we have no sin, we deceive ourselves, and the truth is not in us. If we confess our sins, he who is faithful and just will forgive us our sins and cleanse us from all unrighteousness. If we say that we have not sinned, we make him a liar, and his word is not in us. (1 John 1.8–10)

We know that Christ, being raised from the dead, will never die again; death no longer has dominion over him. The death he died, he died to sin, once for all; but the life he lives, he lives to God. So you also must consider yourselves dead to sin and alive to God in Christ Jesus. (Romans 6.9–11)

'Enter through the narrow gate; for the gate is wide and the road is easy that leads to destruction, and there are many who take it. For the gate is narrow and the road is hard that leads to life, and there are few who find it.' (Matthew 7.13)

The law of the Spirit of life in Christ Jesus has set you free from the law of sin and of death. (Romans 8.2)

Citizens of the Kingdom: God's Love for Us

We know love by this, that he laid down his life for us – and we ought to lay down our lives for one another. (1 John 3.16)

<Beloved,> let us love one another, because love is from God; everyone who loves is born of God and knows God. (1 John 4.7)

Whoever does not love does not know God, for God is love. God's love was revealed among us in this way: God sent his only Son into the world so that we might live through him. (1 John 4.8–9)

<Beloved,> since God loved us so much, we also ought to love one another. No one has ever seen God; if we love one another, God lives in us, and his love is perfected in us. (1 John 4.11–12)

God is love, and those who abide in love abide in God, and God abides in them. (1 John 4.16b)

'For God so loved the world that he gave his only Son, so that everyone who believes in him may not perish but may have eternal life.' (John 3.16)

'By this everyone will know that you are my disciples, if you have love for one another.' (John 13.35)

Jesus answered him, 'Those who love me will keep my word, and my Father will love them, and we will come to them and make our home with them.' (John 14.23)

Citizens of Heaven: Lifestyle

'A good tree cannot bear bad fruit, nor can a bad tree bear good fruit. Every tree that does not bear good fruit is cut down and thrown into the fire. Thus you will know them by their fruits.' (Matthew 7.18–20)

If anyone is in Christ, there is a new creation: everything old passed away; see, everything has become new! (2 Corinthians 5.17)

'You call me Teacher and Lord – and you are right, for that is what I am. So if I, your Lord and Teacher, have washed your feet, you also ought to wash one another's feet.' (John 13.13–14)

He has graciously granted you the privilege not only of believing in Christ, but of suffering for him as well. (Philippians 1.29)

Therefore, <my beloved,> be steadfast, immovable, always excelling in the work of the Lord, because you know that in the Lord your labour is not in vain. (1 Corinthians 15.58)

Listen! I am standing at the door, knocking; if you hear my voice and open the door, I will come in to you and eat with you, and you with me. (Revelation 3.20)

Citizens of Heaven: God's Spirit

If the Spirit of him who raised Jesus from the dead dwells in you, he who raised Christ from the dead will give life to your mortal bodies also through his Spirit that dwells in you. (Romans 8.11)

Let what you heard from the beginning abide in you. If what you heard from the beginning abides in you, then you will abide in the Son and in the Father. And this is what he has promised us, eternal life. (1 John 2.24–25)

By this we know that we abide in him and he in us, because he has given us of his Spirit. (1 John 4.13)

ECUMENICAL

There is one body and one spirit, just as you were called to the one hope of your calling, one Lord, one faith, one baptism, one God and Father of all, who is above all and through all and in all. (Ephesians 4.4–6)

Because there is one bread, we who are many are one body, for we all partake of the one bread. (1 Corinthians 10.17)

You are no longer strangers and aliens, but you are citizens with the saints and also members of the household of God, built upon the foundation of the apostles and prophets, with Christ Jesus himself as the cornerstone. In him the whole structure is joined together and grows into a holy temple in the Lord. (Ephesians 2.19–21)

'For where two or three are gathered in my name, I am there among them.' (Matthew 18.20)

Above all, clothe yourselves with love, which binds everything together in perfect harmony. And let the peace of Christ rule in your hearts, to which indeed you were called in the one body. (Colossians 3.14–15)

From the rising of the sun to its setting my name is great among the nations, and in every place incense is offered to my name, and a pure offering; for my name is great among the nations, says the Lord of hosts. (Malachi 1.11)

FAITH

Old Testament

Commit your way to the Lord; trust him, and he will act. (Psalm 37.5)

Trust in the Lord with all your heart, and do not rely on your own insight. In all your ways acknowledge him, and he will make straight your paths. (Proverbs 3.5–6)

Look at the proud! Their spirit is not right in them, but the righteous live by their faith. (Habakkuk 2.4)

New Testament

'For truly I tell you, if you have faith the size of a mustard seed, you will say to this mountain, "Move from here to there", and it will move; and nothing will be impossible for you.' (Matthew 17.20–21)

'Whatever you ask for in prayer with faith, you will receive.' (Matthew 21.22)

The apostles said to the Lord, 'Increase our faith!' The Lord replied, 'If you had faith the size of a mustard seed, you could say to this mulberry tree, "Be uprooted and planted in the sea", and it would obey you.' (Luke 17.5–6)

'When the Son of Man comes, will he find faith on earth?' (Luke 18.8b)

Therefore, since we are justified by faith, we have peace with God through our Lord Jesus Christ, through whom we have obtained access to this grace in which we stand. (Romans 5.1–2a)

Keep alert, stand firm in your faith, be courageous, be strong. Let all that you do be done in love. (1 Corinthians 16.13)

But now that faith has come, we are no longer subject to a disciplinarian, for in Christ Jesus you are all children of God through faith. (Galatians 3.25–26)

By grace you have been saved through faith, and this is not your own doing; it is the gift of God – not the results of works, so that no one may boast. (Ephesians 2.8–9)

Faith is the assurance of things hoped for, the conviction of things not seen. (Hebrews 11.1)

Be faithful until death, and I will give you the crown of life. (Revelation 2.10b)

GOD

Old Testament

'The Lord is slow to anger, and abounding in steadfast love, forgiving iniquity and transgression.' (Numbers 14.18a)

Surely God is great, and we do not know him; the number of his years is unsearchable. For he draws up the drops of water; he distils his mist in rain, which the skies pour down and drop upon mortals abundantly. (Job 36.26–28)

The Lord tests the righteous and the wicked, and his soul hates the lover of violence. (Psalm 11.5)

The law of the Lord is perfect, reviving the soul; the decrees of the Lord are sure, making wise the simple; the precepts of the Lord are right, rejoicing the heart. (Psalm 19.7–8a)

Good and upright is the Lord; therefore he instructs sinners in the way. (Psalm 25.8)

All the paths of the Lord are steadfast love and faithfulness, for those who keep his covenant and his decrees. (Psalm 25.10)

Your steadfast love, O Lord, extends to the heavens, your faithfulness to the clouds. Your righteousness is like the mighty mountains, your judgements are like the great deep. (Psalm 36.5–6a)

How precious is your steadfast love, O God! All people may take refuge in the shadow of your wings. (Psalm 36.7)

Your throne, O God, endures for ever and ever. Your royal sceptre is a sceptre of equity; you love righteousness and hate wickedness. (Psalm 45.6–7a)

Lord, you have been our dwelling-place in all generations. Before the mountains were brought forth, or ever you had formed the earth and the world, from everlasting to everlasting you are God. (Psalm 90.1–2)

The Lord is king, he is robed in majesty; the Lord is robed, he is girded with strength. He has established the world; it shall never be moved. (Psalm 93.1)

Know that the Lord is God. It is he that made us, and we are his; we are his people, and the sheep of his pasture. (Psalm 100.3)

The Lord is good; his steadfast love endures for ever, and his faithfulness to all generations. (Psalm 100.5)

As a father has compassion for his children, so the Lord has compassion for those who fear him. For he knows how we were made; he remembers that we are dust. (Psalm 103.13–14)

Your name, O Lord, endures for ever, your renown, O Lord, throughout all ages. For the Lord will vindicate his people, and have compassion on his servants. (Psalm 135.13–14)

The Lord is faithful in all his words, and gracious in all his deeds. (Psalm 145.13b)

The Lord sets the prisoners free; the Lord opens the eyes of the blind. The Lord lifts up those who are bowed down. (Psalm 146.7b–8)

The Lord watches over the strangers; he upholds the orphan and the widow. (Psalm 146.9a)

The Lord lifts up the downtrodden; he casts the wicked to the ground. (Psalm 147.6)

The grass withers, the flower fades; but the word of our God will stand for ever. (Isaiah 40.8)

The steadfast love of the Lord never ceases, his mercies never come to an end; they are new every morning; great is your faithfulness. (Lamentations 3.22–23)

The Lord is good to those who wait for him, to the soul that seeks him. It is good that one should wait quietly for the salvation of the Lord. (Lamentations 3.25–26)

I myself will be the shepherd of my sheep, and I will make them lie down, says the Lord God. I will seek the lost, and I will bring back the strayed, and I will bind up the injured, and I will strengthen the weak. (Ezekiel 34.15–16a)

You are my sheep, the sheep of my pasture, and I am your God, says the Lord God. (Ezekiel 34.31)

New Testament

'God so loved the world that he gave his only Son, so that everyone who believes in him may not perish but may have eternal life.' (John 3.16)

'Indeed, God did not send the Son into the world to condemn the world, but in order that the world might be saved through him.' (John 3.17)

'God is a spirit, and those who worship him must worship in spirit and truth.' (John 4.24)

God proves his love for us in that while we still were sinners Christ died for us. (Romans 5.8)

For if while we were enemies, we were reconciled to God through the death of his Son, much more surely, having been reconciled, will we be saved by his life. (Romans 5.10)

If God is for us, who is against us? He who did not withhold his own Son, but gave him up for all of us, will he not with him also give us everything else? (Romans 8.31b–32)

The sting of death is sin, and the power of sin is the law. But thanks be to God, who gives us the victory through our Lord Jesus Christ. (1 Corinthians 15.56–57)

Blessed be the God and Father of our Lord Jesus Christ, the Father of mercies and the God of all consolation, who consoles us in all our affliction. (2 Corinthians 1.3–4a)

The word of God is living and active, sharper than any two-edged sword, piercing until it divides soul from spirit, joints from marrow; it is able to judge the thoughts and intentions of the heart. (Hebrews 4.12)

God is love, and those who abide in love abide in God, and God abides in them. (1 John 4.16b)

'I am the Alpha and the Omega', says the Lord God, who is and who was and who is to come, the Almighty. (Revelation 1.8)

Old Testament

In the beginning when God created the heavens and the earth, the earth was a formless void and darkness covered the face of the deep, while a wind from God swept over the face of the waters. (Genesis 1.1–2)

So Moses went out and told the people the words of the Lord; and he gathered seventy elders of the people, and placed them all around the tent. Then the Lord came down in the cloud and spoke to him, and took some of the spirit that was on him and put it on the seventy elders; and when the spirit rested upon them, they prophesied. (Numbers 11.24–25)

The Lord said to Moses, 'Take Joshua son of Nun, a man in whom is the spirit, and lay your hand upon him; have him stand before Eleazar the priest and all the congregation, and commission him in their sight.' (Numbers 27.18–19)

The woman bore a son, and named him Samson. The boy grew, and the Lord blessed him. The spirit of the Lord began to stir him. (Judges 13.24–25a)

New Testament

Now the birth of Jesus the Messiah took place in this way. When his mother Mary had been engaged to

Joseph, but before they lived together, she was found to be with child from the Holy Spirit. (Matthew 1.18)

And when Jesus had been baptized, just as he came up from the water, suddenly the heavens were opened to him and he saw the Spirit of God descending like a dove and alighting on him. (Matthew 3.16)

Then Jesus was led up by the Spirit into the wilderness to be tempted by the devil. (Matthew 4.1)

At that time Jesus said, 'I thank you, Father, Lord of heaven and earth, because you have hidden these things from the wise and the intelligent and have revealed them to infants; yes, Father, for such was your gracious will.' (Matthew 11.25–26)

And John testified, 'I saw the Spirit descending from heaven like a dove, and it remained on him. I myself did not know him, but the one who sent me to baptize with water said to me, "He on whom you see the Spirit descend and remain is the one who baptizes with the Holy Spirit."' (John 1.32–34)

[Jesus said] 'If you love me, you will keep my commandments. And I will ask the Father, and he will give you another Advocate, to be with you for ever. This is the Spirit of truth, whom the world cannot receive, because it neither sees him nor knows him. You know him, because he abides with you, and he will be in you.' (John 14.15–17)

[Jesus said] 'The Advocate, the Holy Spirit, whom the Father will send in my name, will teach you everything, and remind you of all that I have said to you.' (John 14.26)

[Jesus said] 'When the Spirit of truth comes, he will guide you into all the truth; for he will not speak on his own, but will speak whatever he hears, and he will declare to you the things that are to come.' (John 16.13)

When they had prayed, the place in which they were gathered together was shaken; and they were all filled with the Holy Spirit and spoke the word of God with boldness. (Acts 4.31)

God's love has been poured into our hearts through the Holy Spirit that has been given to us. (Romans 5.5b)

The Spirit helps us in our weakness; for we do not know how to pray as we ought, but that very Spirit intercedes with sighs too deep for words. (Romans 8.26)

God, who searches the heart, knows what is the mind of the Spirit, because the Spirit intercedes for the saints according to the will of God. (Romans 8.27)

The fruit of the Spirit is love, joy, peace, patience, kindness, generosity, faithfulness, gentleness, and self-control. (Galatians 5.22–23a)

The Spirit searches everything, even the depths of God. For what human being knows what is truly human except the human spirit that is within? So also no one comprehends what is truly God's except the Spirit of God. (1 Corinthians 2.10b–12)

Do you not know that your body is a temple of the Holy Spirit within you, which you have from God, and that you are not your own? (1 Corinthians 6.19)

No one speaking by the Spirit of God ever says 'Let Jesus be cursed!' and no one can say 'Jesus is Lord' except by the Holy Spirit. (1 Corinthians 12.3)

Now there are varieties of gifts, but the same Spirit; and there are varieties of services, but the same Lord. (1 Corinthians 12.4–5)

To each is given the manifestation of the Spirit for the common good. To one is given through the Spirit the utterance of wisdom, and to another the utterance of knowledge according to the same Spirit, to another faith by the same Spirit, to another gifts of healing by the one Spirit, to another the working of miracles, to another prophecy, to another the discernment of spirits, to another various kinds of tongues, to another the interpretation of tongues. (1 Corinthians 12.7–10)

It is God who establishes us with you in Christ and has anointed us, by putting his seal on us and giving us his Spirit in our hearts as a first instalment. (2 Corinthians 1.21–22)

The Lord is the Spirit, and where the Spirit of the Lord is, there is freedom. (2 Corinthians 3.17)

By this we know that we abide in him and he in us, because he has given us of his Spirit. (1 John 4.13)

JESUS

Old Testament: Prophecy

The stone that the builders rejected has become the chief cornerstone. This is the Lord's doing; it is marvellous in our eyes. (Psalm 118.22–23)

The Lord himself will give you a sign. Look, the young woman is with child and shall bear a son, and shall name him Immanuel. (Isaiah 7.14)

The people who walked in darkness have seen a great light; those who lived in a land of deep darkness – on them light has shined. (Isaiah 9.2)

For a child has been born for us, a son given to us; authority rests upon his shoulders; and he is named Wonderful Counsellor, Mighty God, Everlasting Father, Prince of Peace. (Isaiah 9.6)

A shoot shall come out from the stock of Jesse, and a branch shall grow out of his roots. The spirit of the Lord shall rest on him, the spirit of wisdom and understanding, the spirit of counsel and might, the spirit of knowledge and the fear of the Lord. (Isaiah 11.1–2)

The root of Jesse shall stand as a signal to the peoples; the nations shall inquire of him, and his dwelling shall be glorious. (Isaiah 11.10)

Arise, shine; for your light has come, and the glory of the Lord has risen upon you. (Isaiah 60.1)

The Word

In the beginning was the Word, and the Word was with God, and the Word was God. He was in the beginning with God. (John 1.1)

The light shines in the darkness, and the darkness did not overcome it. (John 1.5)

And the Word became flesh and lived among us, and we have seen his glory, the glory as of a father's only son, full of grace and truth. (John 1.14)

Jesus: Birth

In the sixth month the angel Gabriel was sent by God to a town in Galilee called Nazareth, to a virgin engaged to a man whose name was Joseph, of the house of David. The virgin's name was Mary. (Luke 1.26–27)

And Mary said, 'My soul magnifies the Lord, and my spirit rejoices in God my Saviour, for he has looked with favour on the lowliness of his servant.' (Luke 1.46–48)

But the angel said to them, 'Do not be afraid; for see – I am bringing you good news of great joy for all the people: to you is born this day in the city of David a Saviour, who is the Messiah, the Lord.' (Luke 2.10–11)

And suddenly there was with the angel a multitude of the heavenly host, praising God and saying, 'Glory to God in the highest heaven, and on earth peace among those whom he favours!' (Luke 2.13–14)

When the angels had left them and gone into heaven, the shepherds said to one another, 'Let us go now to Bethlehem and see this thing that has taken place, which the Lord has made known to us.' (Luke 2.15)

They went with haste and found Mary and Joseph, and the child lying in the manger. (Luke 2.16)

Mary treasured all these words and pondered them in her heart. The shepherds returned, glorifying and praising God for all they had heard and seen, as it had been told them. (Luke 2.19–20)

After eight days had passed, it was time to circumcise the child; and he was called Jesus, the name given by the angel. (Luke 2.21)

The child grew and became strong, filled with wisdom; and the favour of God was upon him. (Luke 2.40)

Jesus: Baptism

Jesus came from Galilee to John at the Jordan, to be baptized by him. (Matthew 3.13)

When Jesus had been baptized, just as he came up from the water, suddenly the heavens were opened to him and he saw the Spirit of God descending like a dove and alighting on him. (Matthew 3.16)

And a voice from heaven said, 'This is my Son, the Beloved, with whom I am well pleased.' (Matthew 3.17)

Jesus: Teaching

Now when Jesus had finished saying these things, the crowds were astounded at his teaching, for he taught them as one having authority, and not as their scribes. (Matthew 7.28–29)

They were astounded beyond measure, saying, 'He has done everything well; he even makes the deaf to hear and the mute to speak.' (Mark 7.37)

Jesus called the twelve together and gave them power and authority over all demons and to cure diseases, and he sent them out to proclaim the kingdom of God and to heal. (Luke 9.1–2)

Jesus said to them, 'I am the bread of life. Whoever comes to me will never be hungry, and whoever believes in me will never be thirsty.' (John 6.35)

While Jesus was standing there, he cried out, 'Let anyone who is thirsty come to me, and let the one who believes in me drink.' (John 7.37b–38a)

Jesus spoke to them, saying, 'I am the light of the world. Whoever follows me will never walk in darkness but will have the light of life.' (John 8.12)

Jesus said, 'I came into this world for judgement so that those who do not see may see, and those who do see may become blind.' (John 9.39)

Then Jesus cried aloud: 'Whoever believes in me believes not in me but in him who sent me. And whoever sees me sees him who sent me.' (John 12.44–45)

Jesus: Welcome into Jerusalem

The crowd that had come to the festival heard that Jesus was coming to Jerusalem. So they took branches of palm trees and went out to meet him, shouting, 'Hosanna! Blessed is the one who comes in the name of the Lord – the King of Israel!' (John 12.12–13)

Jesus found a young donkey and sat on it; as it is written: 'Do not be afraid, daughter of Zion. Look, your king is coming, sitting on a donkey's colt!' (John 12.14–15)

Jesus sent two disciples, saying to them, 'Go into the village ahead of you, and immediately you will find a donkey tied, and a colt with her; untie them and bring them to me. If anyone says anything to you, just say this, "The Lord needs them."' (Matthew 21.1b–3a)

Jesus: The Last Supper

Jesus sent Peter and John, saying, 'Go and prepare the Passover meal for us that we may eat it.' (Luke 22.8)

The Lord Jesus on the night when he was betrayed took a loaf of bread, and when he had given thanks, he broke it and said, 'This is my body that is for you. Do this in remembrance of me.' (1 Corinthians 11.23b–24)

In the same way he took the cup also, after supper, saying, 'This cup is the new covenant in my blood. Do this, as often as you drink it, in remembrance of me.' (1 Corinthians 11.25)

Jesus: Suffering and Death

Pilate asked them, 'Shall I crucify your King?' The chief priests answered, 'We have no king but the emperor.' Then he handed him over to them to be crucified. (John 19.15b–16)

Jesus said, 'Father, forgive them; for they do not know what they are doing.' (Luke 23.34)

It was now about noon, and darkness came over the whole land until three in the afternoon, while the sun's light failed; and the curtain of the temple was torn in two. (Luke 23.44–45)

Then Jesus, crying with a loud voice, said, 'Father, into your hands I commend my spirit.' Having said this, he breathed his last. (Luke 23.46)

There was a good and righteous man named Joseph, who, though a member of the council, had not agreed to their plan and action. He came from the Jewish town of Arimathea, and he was waiting expectantly for the kingdom of God. This man went to Pilate and asked for the body of Jesus. Then he took it down, wrapped it in a linen cloth, and laid it in a rock-hewn tomb where no one had ever been laid. (Luke 23.50–53)

Jesus: Resurrection

And very early on the first day of the week, when the sun had risen, they [the women] went to the tomb. They had been saying to one another, 'Who will roll away the stone for us from the entrance to the tomb?' When they looked up, they saw that the stone, which was very large, had already been rolled back. (Mark 16.2–4)

After the sabbath, as the first day of the week was dawning, Mary Magdalene and the other Mary went to see the tomb. (Matthew 28.1)

When it was evening on that day, the first day of the week, and the doors of the house where the disciples had met were locked for fear of the Jews, Jesus came and stood among them and said, 'Peace be with you.' (John 20.19)

Then the disciples rejoiced when they saw the Lord. Jesus said to them again, 'Peace be with you.' (John 20.20b–21a)

Jesus: Son of God Brings Salvation

No one has ever seen God. It is God the only Son, who is close to the Father's heart, who has made him known. (John 1.18)

'For God so loved the world that he gave his only Son, so that everyone who believes in him may not perish but may have eternal life.' (John 3.16)

'Indeed, God did not send the Son into the world to condemn the world, but in order that the world might be saved through him.' (John 3.17)

Jesus said to them, 'Very truly, I tell you, unless you eat the flesh of the Son of Man and drink his blood, you have no life in you. Those who eat my flesh and drink my blood have eternal life, and I will raise them up on the last day; for my flesh is true food and my blood is true drink. Those who eat my flesh and drink my blood abide in me, and I in them.' (John 6.53–56)

God proves his love for us in that while we still were sinners Christ died for us. (Romans 5.8)

It is Christ Jesus, who died, yes, who was raised, who is at the right hand of God, who indeed intercedes for us. (Romans 8.34b)

Who will separate us from the love of Christ? Will hardship, or distress, or persecution, or famine, or nakedness, or peril, or sword? (Romans 8.35)

Neither death, nor life, nor angels, nor rulers, nor things present, nor things to come, nor powers, nor height, nor depth, nor anything else in all creation, will be able to separate us from the love of God in Christ Jesus our Lord. (Romans 8.38–39)

Christ has been raised from the dead, the first fruits of those who have died. For since death came through a human being, the resurrection of the dead has also come through a human being. (1 Corinthians 15.20–21)

As all die in Adam, so all will be made alive in Christ. But each in his own order: Christ the first fruits, then at his coming those who belong to Christ. (1 Corinthians 15.22–23)

There is one God; there is also one mediator between God and humankind, Christ Jesus, himself human, who gave himself a ransom for all. (1 Timothy 2.5–6a)

Since, then, we have a great high priest who has passed through the heavens, Jesus, the Son of God, let us hold fast to our confession. (Hebrews 4.14)

Christ did not glorify himself in becoming a high priest, but was appointed by the one who said to him, 'You are my Son, today I have begotten you.' (Hebrews 5.5–6a)

Jesus Christ is the same yesterday and today and for ever. (Hebrews 13.8)

God's love was revealed among us in this way: God sent his only Son into the world so that we might live through him. (1 John 4.9)

In this is love, not that we loved God but that he loved us and sent his Son to be the atoning sacrifice for our sins. (1 John 4.10)

God abides in those who confess that Jesus is the Son of God, and they abide in God. So we have known and believe. (1 John 4.15–16a)

Everyone who believes that Jesus is the Christ has been born of God. (1 John 5.1a)

Old Testament

Honour your father and your mother, so that your days may be long in the land that the Lord your God is giving you. (Exodus 20.12)

You shall not make wrongful use of the name of the Lord your God, for the Lord will not acquit anyone who misuses his name. (Deuteronomy 5.11)

Observe the sabbath day and keep it holy, as the Lord your God commanded you. For six days you shall labour and do all your work. But the seventh day is a sabbath to the Lord your God; you shall not do any work. (Deuteronomy 5.12–14a)

What does the Lord your God require of you? Only to fear the Lord your God, to walk in all his ways, to love him, to serve the Lord your God with all your heart and with all your soul, and to keep the commandments of the Lord your God and his decrees. (Deuteronomy 10.12–13a)

Commit your way to the Lord; trust him, and he will act. (Psalm 37.5)

Happy are those who consider the poor; the Lord delivers them in the day of trouble. (Psalm 41.1)

Happy are those whose way is blameless, who walk in the law of the Lord. Happy are those who keep his decrees, who seek him with their whole heart, who also do no wrong, but walk in his ways. (Psalm 119.1)

Unless the Lord builds the house, those who build it labour in vain. (Psalm 127.1a)

Happy is everyone who fears the Lord, who walks in his ways. (Psalm 128.1)

The fear of the Lord is the beginning of knowledge; fools despise wisdom and instruction. (Proverbs 1.7)

The fear of the Lord is instruction in wisdom, and humility goes before honour. (Proverbs 15.33)

Whoever is kind to the poor lends to the Lord, and will be repaid in full. (Proverbs 19.17)

Whoever pursues righteousness and kindness will find life and honour. (Proverbs 21.21)

The Lord is good to those who wait for him, to the soul that seeks him. It is good that one should wait quietly for the salvation of the Lord. (Lamentations 3.25–26)

Seek good and not evil, that you may live; and so the Lord, the God of hosts, will be with you. (Amos 5.14)

The Lord is just in all the works that he has commanded us to do. Yet we have not obeyed his voice, to walk in the statutes of the Lord that he set before us. (Baruch 2.9b–10)

New Testament

'Ask, and it will be given to you; search, and you will find; knock, and the door will be opened for you.' (Matthew 7.7)

'In everything do to others as you would have them do to you; for this is the law and the prophets.' (Matthew 7.12)

'Do not work for the food that perishes, but for the food that endures for eternal life, which the Son of Man will give you.' (John 6.27)

Let love be genuine; hate what is evil, hold fast to what is good; love one another with mutual affection; outdo one another in showing honour. Do not lag in zeal, be ardent in spirit, serve the Lord. (Romans 12.9–11)

Rejoice in hope, be patient in suffering, persevere in prayer. Contribute to the needs of the saints; extend hospitality to strangers. (Romans 12.12–13)

Bless those who persecute you; bless and do not curse them. Rejoice with those who rejoice, weep with those who weep. Live in harmony with one another. (Romans 12.14–16a)

Pay to all what is due to them – taxes to whom taxes are due, revenue to whom revenue is due, respect to whom respect is due, honour to whom honour is due. (Romans 13.7)

Owe no one anything, except to love one another; for the one who loves another has fulf
(Romans 13.8)

Love is patient; love is kind; love is not envious or boastful or arrogant or rude. It does
its own way; it is not irritable or resentful; it does not rejoice in wrongdoing, but rejoice:
(1 Corinthians 13.4–6)

Keep alert, stand firm in your faith, be courageous, be strong. Let all that you do be done in love.
(1 Corinthians 16.13–14)

As you therefore have received Christ Jesus the Lord, continue to live your lives in him, rooted and built
up in him and established in the faith, just as you were taught, abounding in thanksgiving. (Colossians
2.6–7)

So if you have been raised with Christ, seek the things that are above, where Christ is, seated at the right
hand of God. (Colossians 3.1)

Set your minds on things that are above, not on things that are on earth, for you have died, and your
life is hidden with Christ in God. When Christ who is your life is revealed, then you also will be revealed
with him in glory. (Colossians 3.2–4)

As God's chosen ones, holy and beloved, clothe yourselves with compassion, kindness, humility, meekness,
and patience. (Colossians 3.12)

.othe yourselves with love, which binds everything together in perfect harmony. And let the peace of Christ rule in your hearts, to which indeed you were called in the one body. (Colossians 3.14–15)

Let the word of Christ dwell in you richly; teach and admonish one another in all wisdom; and with gratitude in your hearts sing psalms, hymns, and spiritual songs to God. (Colossians 3.16)

Whatever you do, in word or deed, do everything in the name of the Lord Jesus, giving thanks to God the Father through him. (Colossians 3.17)

Rejoice always, pray without ceasing, give thanks in all circumstances; for this is the will of God in Christ Jesus for you. (1 Thessalonians 5.16–18)

If we have died with him, we will also live with him; if we endure, we will also reign with him; if we deny him, he will also deny us; if we are faithless, he remains faithful. (2 Timothy 2.11b–13a)

Whoever says, 'I am in the light', while hating a brother or sister, is still in the darkness. Whoever loves a brother or sister lives in the light, and in such a person there is no cause for stumbling. But whoever hates another believer is in the darkness, walks in the darkness, and does not know the way to go, because the darkness has brought on blindness. (1 John 2.9–11)

We know love by this, that he laid down his life for us – and we ought to lay down our lives for one another. (1 John 3.16)

Old Testament

All the ends of the earth shall remember and turn to the Lord; and all the families of the nations shall worship before him. (Psalm 22.27)

May God be gracious to us and bless us and make his face to shine upon us, that your way may be known upon earth, your saving power among all nations. (Psalm 67.1–2)

Declare his glory among the nations, his marvellous works among all the peoples. (Psalm 96.3)

Give thanks to the Lord, call on his name; make known his deeds among the nations; proclaim that his name is exalted. (Isaiah 12.4b)

Sing praises to the Lord, for he has done gloriously; let this be known in all the earth. Shout aloud and sing for joy. (Isaiah 12.5–6a)

And the Lord will become king over all the earth; on that the day the Lord will be one and his name one. (Zechariah 14.9)

New Testament

Jesus began to proclaim, 'Repent, for the kingdom of heaven has come near.' As he walked by the Sea of Galilee, he saw two brothers, Simon, who is called Peter, and Andrew his brother, casting a net into the lake – for they were fishermen. And he said to them, 'Follow me, and I will make you fish for people.' (Matthew 4.17–20)

'Let your light shine before others, so that they may see your good works and give glory to your Father in heaven.' (Matthew 5.16)

'Those who are well have no need of a physician, but those who are sick. Go and learn what this means, "I desire mercy, not sacrifice."' (Matthew 9.12–13a)

'The harvest is plentiful, but the labourers are few; therefore ask the Lord of the harvest to send out labourers into his harvest.' (Matthew 9.37–38)

'Proclaim the good news, "The kingdom of heaven has come near."' (Matthew 10.7)

Jesus told his disciples, 'If any want to become my followers, let them deny themselves and take up their cross and follow me.' (Matthew 16.24)

And Jesus came and said to them, 'All authority in heaven and on earth has been given to me. Go therefore and make disciples of all nations, baptizing them in the name of the Father and of the Son and of the Holy Spirit, and teaching them to obey everything that I have commanded you.' (Matthew 28.18–20a)

Jesus said to them, 'Follow me and I will make you fish for people.' (Mark 1.17)

[Jesus] said to them, 'Go into all the world and proclaim the good news, to the whole creation. The one who believes and is baptized will be saved; but the one who does not believe will be condemned.' (Mark 16.15–16)

'And these signs will accompany those who believe: by using my name they will cast out demons; they will speak in new tongues; they will pick up snakes in their hands, and if they drink any deadly thing, it will not hurt them; they will lay their hand on the sick, and they will recover.' (Mark 16.17–18)

'Thus it is written, that the Messiah is to suffer and to rise from the dead on the third day, and that repentance and forgiveness of sins is to be proclaimed in his name to all nations.' (Luke 24.46–47)

'Look around you, and see how the fields are ripe for harvesting. The reaper is already receiving wages and is gathering fruit for eternal life, so that the sower and reaper may rejoice together.' (John 4.35b–36)

Jesus said to Simon Peter, 'Simon son of John, do you love me more than these?' He said to him, 'Yes, Lord; you know that I love you.' Jesus said to him, 'Feed my lambs.' (John 21.15)

Repent, and be baptized every one of you in the name of Jesus Christ so that your sins may be forgiven; and you will receive the gift of the Holy Spirit. (Acts 2.38)

In the presence of God and of Christ Jesus, who is to judge the living and the dead, and in view of his appearing and his kingdom, I solemnly urge you: proclaim the message; be persistent whether the time is favourable or unfavourable, convince, rebuke, and encourage, with the utmost patience in teaching. (2 Timothy 4.1–2)

Be sober, endure suffering, do the work of an evangelist, carry out your ministry fully. (2 Timothy 4.5b)

Old Testament

O give thanks to the Lord, call on his name, make known his deeds among the peoples. Sing to him, sing praises to him, tell of all his wonderful works. (1 Chronicles 16.8–9)

Sing to the Lord, all the earth. Tell of his salvation from day to day. Declare his glory among the nations, his marvellous works among all the peoples. For great is the Lord, and greatly to be praised; he is to be revered above all gods. (1 Chronicles 16.23–25)

Let the heavens be glad, and let the earth rejoice, and let them say among the nations, 'The Lord is King!' Let the sea roar, and all that fills it; let the field exult, and everything in it. (1 Chronicles 16.31–32)

O give thanks to the Lord, for he is good; for his steadfast love endures for ever. (1 Chronicles 16.34)

Yours, O Lord, are the greatness, the power, the glory, the victory, and the majesty; for all that is in the heavens and on the earth is yours. (1 Chronicles 29.11)

O Lord, our Sovereign, how majestic is your name in all the earth! (Psalm 8.9)

Sing praises to the Lord, who dwells in Zion. Declare his deeds among the peoples. (Psalm 9.11)

The heavens are telling the glory of God; and the firmament proclaims his handiwork. (Psalm 19.1)

Blessed be the Lord, for he has wondrously shown his steadfast love. (Psalm 31.21)

Be glad in the Lord and rejoice, O righteous, and shout for joy, all you upright in heart. (Psalm 32.11)

'Great is the Lord, who delights in the welfare of his servant.' (Psalm 35.27b)

How precious is your steadfast love, O God! All people may take refuge in the shadow of your wings. (Psalm 36.7)

Blessed be the Lord, the God of Israel, from everlasting to everlasting. Amen and Amen. (Psalm 41.13)

Clap your hands, all you peoples; shout to God with loud songs of joy. For the Lord, the Most High, is awesome, a great king over all the earth. (Psalm 47.1–2)

Sing praises to God, sing praises; sing praises to our King, sing praises. For God is the king of all the earth. (Psalm 47.6–7a)

Great is the Lord and greatly to be praised in the city of our God. (Psalm 48.1)

Praise is due to you, O God, in Zion; and to you shall vows be performed, O you who answer prayer! (Psalm 65.1–2a)

Make a joyful noise to God, all the earth; sing the glory of his name; give to him glorious praise. Say to God, 'How awesome are your deeds!' (Psalm 66.1–3a)

Let the peoples praise you, O God; let all the peoples praise you. (Psalm 67.3)

Let the nations be glad and sing for joy, for you judge the peoples with equity and guide the nations upon earth. (Psalm 67.4)

Sing to God, sing praises to his name; lift up a song to him. (Psalm 68.4)

Sing to God, O kingdoms of the earth; sing praises to the Lord. (Psalm 68.32)

It is good to give thanks to the Lord, to sing praises to your name, O Most High; to declare your steadfast love in the morning, and your faithfulness by night. (Psalm 92.1–2)

O come, let us sing to the Lord; let us make a joyful noise to the rock of our salvation! Let us come into his presence with thanksgiving; let us make a joyful noise to him with songs of praise! (Psalm 95.1–2)

Sing to the Lord, bless his name; tell of his salvation from day to day. Declare his glory among the nations, his marvellous works among all the peoples. (Psalm 96.2–3)

The Lord is King! Let the earth rejoice. (Psalm 97.1)

Rejoice in the Lord, O you righteous, and give thanks to his holy name! (Psalm 97.12)

O sing to the Lord a new song, for he has done marvellous things. (Psalm 98.1)

Make a joyful noise to the Lord, all the earth; break forth into joyous song and sing praises. (Psalm 98.4)

Make a joyful noise to the Lord, all the earth. Worship the Lord with gladness; come into his presence with singing. (Psalm 100.1–2)

Bless the Lord, O you his angels, you mighty ones who do his bidding, obedient to his spoken word. (Psalm 103.20)

Bless the Lord, O my soul. Praise the Lord! (Psalm 104.35b)

O give thanks to the Lord, call on his name, make known his deeds among the peoples. Sing to him, sing praises to him; tell of all his wonderful works. (Psalm 105.1–2)

Praise the Lord! O give thanks to the Lord, for he is good; for his steadfast love endures for ever. (Psalm 106.1)

O give thanks to the Lord, for he is good; for his steadfast love endures for ever. (Psalm 107.1)

Praise the Lord! Praise, O servant of the Lord; praise the name of the Lord. (Psalm 113.1)

Blessed be the name of the Lord from this time on and for evermore. From the rising of the sun to its setting the name of the Lord is to be praised. (Psalm 113.2–3)

Praise the Lord, for the Lord is good; sing to his name, for he is gracious. (Psalm 135.3)

O give thanks to the God of gods, for his steadfast love endures for ever. O give thanks to the Lord of lords, for his steadfast love endures for ever. (Psalm 136.2–3)

Great is the Lord, and greatly to be praised; his greatness is unsearchable. One generation shall laud your works to another, and shall declare your mighty acts. (Psalm 145.3–4)

All your works shall give thanks to you, O Lord, and all your faithful shall bless you. They shall speak of the glory of your kingdom, and tell of your power. (Psalm 145.10–11)

Praise the Lord! How good it is to sing praises to our God; for he is gracious, and a song of praise is fitting. (Psalm 147.1)

Praise the Lord! Praise the Lord from the heavens; praise him in the heights! (Psalm 148.1)

Praise him, you highest heavens, and you waters above the heavens! Let them praise the name of the Lord, for he commanded and they were created. (Psalm 148.4–5)

Praise the Lord! Sing to the Lord a new song, his praise in the assembly of the faithful. (Psalm 149.1)

Sing to the Lord a new song, his praise from the end of the earth! (Isaiah 42.10a)

'Give thanks to the Lord of hosts, for the Lord is good, for his steadfast love endures for ever!' (Jeremiah 33.11b)

'Blessed are you, O God, with every pure blessing; let all your chosen ones bless you. Let them bless you for ever.' (Tobit 8.15b)

New Testament

Now to him who is able to keep you from falling, and to make you stand without blemish in the presence of his glory with rejoicing, to the only God our Saviour, through Jesus Christ our Lord, be glory, majesty, power, and authority, before all time and now and for ever. Amen. (Jude 24–25)

To him who loves us and freed us from our sins by his blood, and made us to be a kingdom, priests serving his God and Father, to him be glory and dominion for ever and ever. Amen. (Revelation 1.5b–6)

'Great and amazing are your deeds, Lord God the Almighty! Just and true are your ways, King of the nations!' (Revelation 15.3b)

'Lord, who will not fear and glorify your name? For you alone are holy. All nations will come and worship before you, for your judgements have been revealed.' (Revelation 15.4)

Old Testament

Light dawns for the righteous, and joy for the upright in heart. Rejoice in the Lord, O you righteous, and give thanks to his holy name! (Psalm 97.11–12)

Let your priests be clothed with righteousness, and let your faithful shout for joy. (Psalm 132.9)

Praise the Lord! Sing to the Lord a new song, his praise in the assembly of the faithful. (Psalm 149.1)

The souls of the righteous are in the hand of God, and no torment will ever touch them. (Wisdom of Solomon 3.1)

The righteous live for ever, and their reward is with the Lord; the most High takes care of them. (Wisdom of Solomon 5.15)

Those who wait for the Lord shall renew their strength, they shall mount up with wings like eagles, they shall run and not be weary, they shall walk and not faint. (Isaiah 40.31)

New Testament

'Blessed rather are those who hear the word of God and obey it!' (Luke 11.28)

[Jesus said] 'You are those who have stood by me in my trials; and I confer on you, just as my Father has conferred on me, a kingdom, so that you may eat and drink at my table in my kingdom, and you will sit on thrones judging the twelve tribes of Israel.' (Luke 22.28)

For since we believe that Jesus died and rose again, even so, through Jesus, God will bring with him those who have died. (1 Thessalonians 4.14)

Then I heard what seemed to be the voice of a great multitude, like the sound of many waters and like the sound of mighty thunder-peals, crying out, 'Hallelujah! For the Lord our God the Almighty reigns.' (Revelation 19.6)

And the angel said to me, 'Write this: Blessed are those who are invited to the marriage supper of the Lamb.' (Revelation 19.9)

SECOND COMING

Old Testament

For darkness shall cover the earth, and thick darkness the peoples; but the Lord will arise upon you, and his glory will appear over you. (Isaiah 60.2)

Look towards the east, O Jerusalem, and see the joy that is coming to you from God. (Baruch 4.36)

Arise, O Jerusalem, stand upon the height; look towards the east, and see your children gathered from west and east at the word of the Holy One, rejoicing that God has remembered them. (Baruch 5.5)

New Testament

'When the Son of Man comes, will he find faith on earth?' (Luke 18.8b)

The Lord comes, who will bring to light the things now hidden in darkness and will disclose the purposes of the heart. Then each one will receive commendation from God. (1 Corinthians 4.5b)

We wait for new heavens and a new earth, where righteousness is at home. (2 Peter 3.13)

Look! He is coming with the clouds; every eye will see him, even those who pierced him; and on his account all the tribes of the earth will wail. So it is to be. Amen. (Revelation 1.7)

And there were loud voices in heaven, saying, 'The kingdom of the world has become the kingdom of our Lord and of his Messiah, and he will reign for ever and ever.' (Revelation 11.15)

The one who testifies to these things says, 'Surely I am coming soon.' Amen. Come, Lord Jesus! (Revelation 22.20)

Old Testament

Let the light of your face shine on us, O Lord! (Psalm 4.6b)

The Lord is a stronghold for the oppressed, a stronghold in times of trouble. (Psalm 9.9)

Rise up, O Lord; O God, lift up your hand; do not forget the oppressed. (Psalm 10.12)

Wait for the Lord; be strong, and let your heart take courage; wait for the Lord! (Psalm 27.14)

O save your people, and bless your heritage; be their shepherd, and carry them for ever. (Psalm 28.9)

Be strong, and let your heart take courage, all you who wait for the Lord. (Psalm 31.24)

God is our refuge and strength, a very present help in trouble. Therefore we will not fear, though the earth should change, though the mountains shake in the heart of the sea; though its waters roar and foam, though the mountains tremble with its tumult. (Psalm 46.1–3)

The Lord of hosts is with us; the God of Jacob is our refuge. (Psalm 46.7)

Cast your burden on the Lord, and he will sustain you. (Psalm 55.22)

How long, O Lord? Will you be angry for ever? Will your jealous wrath burn like fire? (Psalm 79.5)

Do not remember against us the iniquities of our ancestors; let your compassion come speedily to meet us, for we are brought very low. (Psalm 79.8)

Help us, O God of our salvation, for the glory of your name; deliver us, and forgive our sins, for your name's sake. (Psalm 79.9)

Restore us, O God; let your face shine, that we may be saved. (Psalm 80.3)

Restore us, O God of hosts; let your face shine, that we may be saved. (Psalm 80.7)

Restore us again, O God of our salvation, and put away your indignation towards us. Will you be angry with us for ever? Will you prolong your anger to all generations? Will you not revive us again, so that your people may rejoice in you? (Psalm 85.4–6)

How long, O Lord? Will you hide yourself for ever? How long will your wrath burn like fire? (Psalm 89.46)

Our help is in the name of the Lord, who made heaven and earth. (Psalm 124.8)

O Lord, be gracious to us; we wait for you. Be our arm every morning, our salvation in the time of trouble. (Isaiah 33.2)

Then you shall call, and the Lord will answer; you shall cry for help, and he will say, Here I am. (Isaiah 58.9)

The Lord is good, a stronghold on a day of trouble; he protects those who take refuge in him. (Nahum 1.7)

The Lord will give us strength, and light to our eyes. (Baruch 1.12a)

Hear, O Lord, our prayer and supplication, and for your own sake deliver us, and grant us favour. (Baruch 2.14a)

O Lord, look down from your holy dwelling, and consider us. Incline your ear, O Lord, and hear; open your eyes, O Lord, and see. (Baruch 2.16–17a)

O Lord Almighty, <God of Israel,> the soul in anguish and the wearied spirit cry out to you. Hear, O Lord, and have mercy, for we have sinned before you. For you are enthroned for ever, and we are perishing for ever. (Baruch 3.1–3)

Do not remember the iniquities of our ancestors, but in this crisis remember your power and your name. For you are the Lord our God, and it is you, O Lord, whom we will praise. (Baruch 3.5–6)

New Testament

[Jesus said] 'Come to me, all you that are weary and are carrying heavy burdens, and I will give you rest.' (Matthew 11.28)

'Do not let your hearts be troubled. Believe in God.' (John 14.1)

[Jesus said] 'Peace I leave with you; my peace I give to you. I do not give to you as the world gives. Do not let your hearts be troubled, and do not let them be afraid.' (John 14.27)

[Jesus said] 'If you abide in me, and my words abide in you, ask for whatever you wish, and it will be done for you.' (John 15.7)

'If the world hates you, be aware that it hated me before it hated you.' (John 15.18)

'Be strong in the Lord and in the strength of his power.' (Ephesians 6.10)

'Therefore take up the whole armour of God, so that you may be able to withstand on that evil day, and having done everything, to stand firm.' (Ephesians 6.13)

Do not worry about anything, but in everything by prayer and supplication with thanksgiving let your requests be made known to God. And the peace of God, which surpasses all understanding, will guard your hearts and your minds in Christ Jesus. (Philippians 4.6–7)

UNITY

From the rising of the sun to its setting my name is great among the nations, and in every place incense is offered to my name, and a pure offering; for my name is great among the nations, says the Lord of hosts. (Malachi 1.11)

'For where two or three are gathered in my name, I am there among them.' (Matthew 18.20)

Because there is one bread, we who are many are one body, for we all partake of the one bread. (1 Corinthians 10.17)

You are no longer strangers and aliens, but you are citizens with the saints and also members of the household of God, built upon the foundation of the apostles and prophets, with Christ Jesus himself as the cornerstone. In him the whole structure is joined together and grows into a holy temple in the Lord. (Ephesians 2.19–21)

There is one body and one Spirit, just as you were called to the one hope of your calling, one Lord, one faith, one baptism, one God and Father of all, who is above all and through all and in all. (Ephesians 4.4–6)

Above all, clothe yourselves with love, which binds everything together in perfect harmony. And let the peace of Christ rule in your hearts, to which indeed you were called in the one body. (Colossians 3.14–15)

WORSHIP

Old Testament

Blessed shall you be when you come in, and blessed shall you be when you go out. (Deuteronomy 28.6)

[David said] 'May it please you to bless the house of your servant, so that it may continue for ever before you; for you, O Lord God, have spoken, and with your blessing shall the house of your servant be blessed for ever.' (2 Samuel 7.29)

Let the hearts of those who seek the Lord rejoice. Seek the Lord and his strength, seek his presence continually. Remember the wonderful works he has done, his miracles, and the judgements he uttered. (1 Chronicles 16.10b–12)

Ascribe to the Lord the glory due his name; bring an offering, and come before him. Worship the Lord in holy splendour. (1 Chronicles 16.29)

O Lord, let your ear be attentive to the prayer of your servant, and to the prayer of your servants who delight in revering your name. (Nehemiah 1.11)

Let the words of my mouth and the meditation of my heart be acceptable to you, O Lord, my rock and my redeemer. (Psalm 19.14)

Be exalted, O Lord, in your strength! We will sing and praise your power. (Psalm 21.13)

Who shall ascend the hill of the Lord? And who shall stand in his holy place? Those who have clean hands and pure hearts, who do not lift up their souls to what is false, and do not swear deceitfully. (Psalm 24.3–4)

Be strong, and let your heart take courage, all you who wait for the Lord. (Psalm 31.24)

Our soul waits for the Lord; he is our help and shield. Our heart is glad in him, because we trust in his holy name. Let your steadfast love, O Lord, be upon us, even as we hope in you. (Psalm 33.20–22)

Be still before the Lord, and wait patiently for him. (Psalm 37.7a)

Sing to the Lord a new song, his praise from the end of the earth! (Isaiah 42.10a)

Sing praises to God, sing praises; sing praises to our King, sing praises. For God is the king of all the earth; sing praises with a psalm. (Psalm 47.6–7)

We ponder your steadfast love, O God, in the midst of your temple. Your name, O God, like your praise, reaches to the ends of the earth. (Psalm 48.9–10a)

The sacrifice acceptable to God is a broken spirit; a broken and contrite heart, O God, you will not despise. (Psalm 51.17)

How lovely is your dwelling-place, O Lord of hosts! My soul longs, indeed it faints for the courts of the Lord; my heart and my flesh sing for joy to the living God. (Psalm 84.1–2)

Happy are those who live in your house, ever singing your praise. (Psalm 84.4)

It is good to give thanks to the Lord, to sing praises to your name, O Most High; to declare your steadfast love in the morning, and your faithfulness by night. (Psalm 92.1–2)

O come, let us sing to the Lord; let us make a joyful noise to the rock of our salvation! (Psalm 95.1)

Let us come into his presence with thanksgiving; let us make a joyful noise to him with songs of praise! (Psalm 95.2)

O come let us worship and bow down, let us kneel before the Lord our Maker! (Psalm 95.6)

O sing to the Lord a new song; sing to the Lord, all the earth. (Psalm 96.1)

Sing to the Lord, bless his name; tell of his salvation from day to day. Declare his glory among the nations, his marvellous works among all the peoples. (Psalm 96.2–3)

Worship the Lord in holy splendour, tremble before him, all the earth. (Psalm 96.9)

O sing to the Lord a new song, for he has done marvellous things. (Psalm 98.1a)

Make a joyful noise to the Lord, all the earth. Worship the Lord with gladness; come into his presence with singing. (Psalm 100.1–2)

O give thanks to the Lord, call on his name, make known his deeds among the peoples. Sing to him, sing praises to him; tell of all his wonderful works. (Psalm 105.1–2)

This is the gate of the Lord; the righteous shall enter through it. (Psalm 118.20)

This is the day that the Lord has made; let us rejoice and be glad in it. (Psalm 118.24)

Come, bless the Lord, all you servants of the Lord; who stand by night in the house of the Lord! Lift up your hands to the holy place, and bless the Lord. (Psalm 134.1–2)

Praise the Lord! Praise the name of the Lord; give praise, O servants of the Lord, you that stand in the house of the Lord, in the courts of the house of our God. (Psalm 135.1–2)

O Lord, be gracious to us; we wait for you. Be our arm every morning, our salvation in the time of trouble. (Isaiah 33.2)

Seek the Lord while he may be found, call upon him while he is near. (Isaiah 55.6)

New Testament

Jesus answered them, 'Truly I tell you, if you have faith and do not doubt, not only will you do what has been done to the fig tree, but even if you say to this mountain, "Be lifted up and thrown into the sea", it will be done. Whatever you ask for in prayer with faith, you will receive.' (Matthew 21.21–22)

The Spirit helps us in our weakness; for we do not know how to pray as we ought, but that very Spirit intercedes with sighs too deep for words. (Romans 8.26)

Whoever, therefore, eats the bread or drinks the cup of the Lord in an unworthy manner will be answerable for the body and blood of the Lord. Examine yourselves, and only then eat of the bread and drink of the cup. For all who eat and drink without discerning the body, eat and drink judgement against themselves. (1 Corinthians 11.27–29)

Since we have a great priest over the house of God, let us approach with a true heart in full assurance of faith. (Hebrews 10.21–22a)

Since we are receiving a kingdom that cannot be shaken, let us give thanks, by which we offer to God an acceptable worship with reverence and awe. (Hebrews 12.28)

If we say that we have no sin, we deceive ourselves, and the truth is not in us. If we confess our sins, he who is faithful and just will forgive us our sins and cleanse us from all unrighteousness. If we say that we have not sinned, we make him a liar, and his word is not in us. (1 John 1.8–10)

BIBLE INDEX